Ask Harvey,

Harvey W. Schwandner

Harvey W. Schwandner was executive editor of the *Milwaukee Sentinel* when this photograph was taken in 1964, but his skeptical scrutiny of copy is familiar to all of us who worked for him when he was city editor of the *Journal*.

Ask Harvey, pls

by

Edwin R. Bayley

with

former members of the *Milwaukee Journal* staff

PRAIRIE OAK PRESS
Madison, Wisconsin

Prairie Oak Press
821 Prospect Place
Madison, Wisconsin 53703

Typeset by KC Graphics, Inc., Madison, Wisconsin
Printed in the United States of America by BookCrafters,
Chelsea, Michigan

Library of Congress Cataloging-in-Publication Data

Bayley, Edwin R.
　　Ask Harvey, pls / by Edwin R. Bayley, with former members of
the Milwaukee journal staff. -- 1st ed.
　　　　p.　　cm.
　　Includes index.
　　ISBN 1-879483-20-3 : $8.95
　　1. Schwandner, Harvey William, 1908–1988.　2. Journalists --
United States -- 20th Century -- Biography.　3. Editors -- United
States -- 20th century -- Biography.　I. Milwaukee journal.　II. Title.
PN4874.S353B39　　1994
070.4'1'092--dc20
[B]　　　　　　　　　　　　　　　　　　　　　　　94-13249
　　　　　　　　　　　　　　　　　　　　　　　　　　　　CIP

CONTENTS

FOREWORD

Harvey Schwandner was the city editor of the *Milwaukee Journal* from 1946 to 1959, years of the paper's peak influence and steadily rising circulation, when the *Journal* was on every list of the five or ten best newspapers in the country.

Its national reputation was partly a result of the excellence of its editorial page, especially its early, outspoken and courageous opposition to the demagoguery of Senator Joseph R. McCarthy of Wisconsin. Among its peers, however, the *Journal*'s eminence was equally attributable to the thoroughness and quality of its local reporting. For the period after World War II, that was Schwandner's responsibility.

In July of 1990, John D. Pomfret was visiting at our farm in Door County, Wisconsin. We had come there from a reunion of *Journal* news and editorial alumni in Milwaukee and we fell to swapping stories about Harvey. We agreed that he had been an extraordinary man who had played a decisive part in the making of a great paper, who had taught us much and had instilled values and standards that stayed with us all of our lives. It occurred to us that a collection of anecdotes, opinions, prejudices and theories about Harvey might make interesting reading and tell us a lot about newspapers in their last burst of glory before television came to dominate the mass media.

I solicited recollections directly and through former *Journal* editorial writer John H. Thompson's list of *Journal* alumni. I shuffled the reminiscences of the respondents into a narrative. This book is the result.

In the years covered by this narrative, the *Journal*—invariably among the nation's top papers in advertising volume—was also among the most prosperous. In the news department, that was reflected in generous staffing, plenty of overtime and lots of space in the paper for stories.

Morale in the newsroom was high for these reasons and because of the *Journal*'s stock ownership plan, the first of its sort among American newspapers. When Agnes Wahl Nieman, the widow of the *Journal*'s founder, died in 1936, she left her share of *Journal* stock to Harvard University. The university gave its support to a plan for employee stock ownership devised by Harry J. Grant, the *Journal*'s business manager, and sold the stock to his group rather than to outside publishers who had offered more for the shares.

Employees were able to buy units in a trust which owned a majority of the stock. Customarily, they borrowed from the bank at low interest rates—3 per cent in 1950—and paid the interest and amortized their loans with annual dividends that ran 10 to 12 per cent. It was a painless way of saving.

One result was that reporters and editors at the *Journal* tended to stay longer than those elsewhere in their semi-nomadic trade. And, although salaries at the *Journal* were a bit lower than at comparable newspapers, there was a feeling that anyone who left the *Journal* was not only disloyal but financially reckless.

In addition to its substantial financial benefits, the stock plan protected the employees from having their paper sold out from under them.

Some of the conditions that made the afternoon *Journal* an exciting place to work have changed.

In the 1990s, the principal sources of news are morning newspapers and evening television. The growth of the suburbs has forced afternoon papers to roll back deadlines to gain time to distribute papers. The result is that they provide their readers with little but features and day-old news. The morning papers have six to eight hours for distribution and television can cover news as it happens.

Fifty years ago in most cities, afternoon newspapers were dominant. With deadlines in the early afternoon, they could provided detailed, well-written reports of the last night's events and a good serving of fresh news from the first half of today. They could even get out a decent edition for same-day distribution to readers as far away as 150 miles from the metropolis.

The vitality of afternoon papers meant much greater competition than there is today in all but a handful of American cities. In Milwaukee, the battle was between the afternoon *Journal* and Hearst's morning *Sentinel*, with both publishing morning editions on Sundays.

The *Sentinel* was relatively poor, much thinner than the *Journal* and lacked the numbers and depth of the *Journal*'s staff. But it had competent people who relished pulling the *Journal*'s tail. The readers of both papers benefited enormously.

Reporters are paid more today, but my guess is that they don't have as much fun because the competition is less. Competition was always on our minds in those days at the *Milwaukee Journal*, and the fiercest competitor of all was our city editor, Harvey Schwandner.

Harvey William Schwandner was born December 22, 1908, at Brillion Wisconsin.

He was the son of August and Elizabeth Ziegler Schwandner. His father was the superintendent of Brillion's principal industry, a lime kiln.

After graduating from Brillion High School, he attended Lawrence College (now Lawrence University) at Appleton, Wisconsin, in 1928 and 1929. There he took courses in creative writing from Professor Warren Beck, a novelist and authority on William Faulkner. He dropped out of Lawrence for financial reasons at the onset of the Depression.

While in high school, he worked as a printer's devil for the *Brillion News,* a weekly newspaper with a circulation of about nine hundred. After leaving Lawrence, he was employed as editor of the *New Holstein Reporter,* another weekly. New Holstein is about 25 miles from Brillion.

He was hired by the *Journal* in 1930 and was assigned to the night police beat, working from 11 p.m. to 7 a.m. A few months later he became a one-man bureau in suburban Waukesha, where he stayed for several years.

In 1932 he married his high-school sweetheart, Geraldine Peters. They had a son and two daughters.

He was a reporter and feature writer on the city staff until 1945, covering the courts, serving as a rewrite man, and doing what is now called investigative reporting. He was highly regarded for the quality of his reporting and his skill in writing human interest and humorous stories.

In 1945 he was appointed assistant city editor. A year later he was promoted to city editor. He served as city editor until 1959, when he was promoted to assistant managing editor. When the Journal Company acquired the *Milwaukee Sentinel* from the Hearst Corporation in 1962, he became its executive editor. He was made editor of the *Sentinel* in 1966 and retired in 1975.

After retirement, he and his wife divided the year between their homes in Mequon, a suburb of Milwaukee, and Palm Desert, California. He died in Milwaukee of cancer on June 16, 1988, at age 79.

This book would not have been written but for the help and encouragement of John Pomfret, who was there at the inception, and who edited the manuscript, reorganized it, and indexed it. Nor could it have been written without the cooperation of so many of my former colleagues on the *Journal* staff, who took the time and the effort to sift their memories for the stories and judgments that make up the substance of the book. Brief biographies of them appear in the back of the book. That so many would take the time to set down their memories of Harvey and that those memories are still vivid after so many years is the best evidence of the impact he had on our lives.

Edwin R. Bayley

Carmel, California
March, 1994

A note on the text: Inevitably in a book consisting largely of first person recollections by many contributors, "I" appears often. It will lessen the risk of confusion if the reader will remember that "I" in plain text and not part of quoted material is the voice of the author. Except for very short ones, the anecdotes—the author's, too—are indented and set in a different type face (like this). Introductory phrases and, for longer anecdotes, marginal identifications, make clearer who is talking.

Chapter One

ANXIETY

For more than 30 years I have had anxiety dreams in which I have somehow failed to live up to Harvey Schwandner's standards and expectations. Sometimes I am writing on deadline and I don't have the information that I need to finish the story. Harvey is standing next to me waiting for it. Sometimes I am out on assignment and I can't find a telephone or I can't remember where I parked my car and I've got to get back to the office right away. I have programmed myself to wake up when I am in the grip of one of those dreams; my subconscious has learned how to exorcise them.

James C. Spaulding and John Pomfret have had similar dreams, and I suspect that there are others. John says that as a new reporter, he would dream that he had made a mistake in a story. He would wake up sweating and would have to climb out of bed and look at the paper to reassure himself before he could get back to sleep. For many years after he left the paper he would dream that he was back, but could no longer do the work to Harvey's satisfaction. No one rebuked him; he just stopped getting assignments.

The intensity and persistence of such apprehensions are strange. Neither Jim nor I nor John (once he graduated from writing obituaries) nor most of the others who contributed to this project experienced much of the harassment that Harvey dished out to new reporters. I do not recall being on the receiving end of any of his tantrums and I got my share of the prized notes saying something good about a story that I had written.

Why did we worry so much?

For most of us those were not carefree days. We had come to the paper as survivors of World War II. We had grown up during the Depression and had inherited our parents' insecurities. We had young families, big mortgages and few savings. We liked and valued our jobs. Competition was fierce for slots on good newspapers. An editor could fire you pretty much whenever he felt like it. I saw it happen more than once. At a non-Guild shop like the *Journal* an editor did not even have to prove to an arbitrator that there was just cause for termination.

In reality, though, we did not worry much about being fired. Few were fired and it usually was clear that they deserved it.

I think that it was Harvey's own intensity that created the palpable tension in the *Journal* city room. Coupled with his intensity was a quixotic sense of humor that kept most reporters off balance. You often weren't sure whether he was kidding or not.

Harvey wanted to produce a paper full of stories that were accurate, complete, well-written and lively. And he wanted to win. He wanted to have every story first—to beat the *Sentinel*, the radio and television stations, the *Chicago Tribune* and any other newspaper that had the audacity to send reporters to Milwaukee. He was driven—the Vince Lombardi of newspapers—and he drove us. We worked like dogs.

Two respondents—Carl Eifert and Larry Lohmann—said that they had lived in constant fear.

"I was so uncomfortable working for him that I looked forward to being fired," Lohmann recalled.

"Harvey scared the hell out of me," said Eifert.
Lohmann wrote:

I started at the *Journal* in 1951. Fortunately, in my
first few years, I spent a lot of time out of the office,
first on night police and then on the federal run for four
years. Both were miserable runs with few good stories. But I was thankful to be out of Harvey's reach. I
recall slinking into work, handing in my stories and
dashing over to the federal building before Harvey
could catch me. I was afraid to hand in stories when
Harvey was on the desk and was relieved when his
assistant, [William] Radloff was working in his place.

There were those early morning telephone calls
on my days off, either from Harvey or one of the
rewrite men saying, "Harvey wants to know . . ."
to plug holes in my stories. In my weakened state
of mind, I suspected those calls were calculated
to harass me. Was he trying to get me to quit? I
was tempted to look elsewhere, but jobs on good
papers were scarce. I stuck it out even though I was
miserable.

Later, covering the suburbs, my misery lessened.
Perhaps I was getting used to Harvey, but I still
worked in fear. I realized that Harvey was tough on
other reporters, too. But I also observed that most of
them were better able to take it than I was. Or they
moved to other jobs on the paper. George Lockwood,
I'm convinced, moved to the roto section to get away
from Harvey. I continued on the city side, although
feeling that I was way over my head.

Of course, I recognized that Harvey was a good
city editor. However, I believe that Rod Van Every was
as good and easier to work for. The knowledge that
Harvey was under great pressure and had a short
fuse did not really make things easier for me.

I wonder whether a city/metro editor today could
be another Harvey—a really strong city editor. I doubt
if today's reporters would work long in the face of

anger such as Harvey's. They seem to be ready to move to lesser papers, like Dallas, for much less than that, perhaps because the *Journal* is not the paper it used to be.

That, of course, is the view of an old-timer who thinks that a lot of things are going downhill.

Carl Eifert came to the *Journal* as an experienced newspaperman. His first assignment was on rewrite, working right at Harvey's elbow. He wrote:

I saw a lot of Harvey close up. One of my tasks was to get the weather forecast at a certain time each morning. As I recall, I was always late, even though I assiduously called the Weather Bureau each day at the appointed time. Harvey would give me hell for missing the deadline, yet the forecast would always show up in the paper. He never did tell me but I accidentally discovered that I had been calling later than I should have.

Eifert said that despite his fear of Harvey he considered Schwandner "a great editor and a good man." He enjoyed Harvey's humor after he was transferred to the state desk and was out of the direct line of fire.

Less forgiving was Louise Cattoi. She was in her nineties when she wrote these comments:

I resented Harvey's difficult and jabbing personality. I was happy when his reign ended. It wasn't that he shirked or did not do his job. It was his personality that was a problem. He could fill a reporter with inner and outer resentment. He was prickly. I suppose that inside he was a pretty nice guy, but the overall stance was prickly.

The women who responded were generally less enthusiastic about Harvey than the men. Elizabeth (Liz) Block Wing wondered about his underlying attitude toward women:

From my current perspective, I think his sexism was no more or less than that of most other males in the *Journal* city room of the early to mid-'50s. But his use of his authority as city editor made it seem [more] so at the time.

Laura Pilarski had this to say:

Harvey was not an easy person to deal with. He terrified some reporters—Louise Cattoi, for one. My basic attitude was to keep my distance and speak sparingly to Harvey. But I do give him credit for helping to mold a newspaper that editorially was tops. What I learned under Harvey's sometimes harsh guidance has benefited me as a journalist to this day.

Ellen Gibson Wilson wrote:

I cannot recall tangling with Harvey, but I remember him as someone to steer clear of. I know he was critical at times, but he also offered occasional, brief praise, I think. I didn't really like him, to be honest, nor did I feel he had much vision.

Viola (Vi) Dewey said:

I just remember Harvey for his sarcastic wit and his moral support.

Merrick S. (Rick) Wing said that when Liz Block, whom he later married, first met Harvey, she thought he was a mild, kindly gentleman. But she soon came to fear him because as a beginner she made mistakes. "Even when Harvey complimented her on a story, as he occasionally did, she was terrified of what he would criticize next," he wrote. Liz said that Harvey seldom, if ever, took the time to be a teacher or to train a new employee.

Pomfret recalled an effort to teach him:

I hadn't written for a newspaper before I joined the *Journal* staff. I soon developed a serviceable enough style for hard news stories, but the feature touch eluded me. Schwandner had been a superb feature writer and tried hard to get me to loosen up. His efforts were unavailing. One day he said in frustration: "Pomfret, you ought to read more trash."

John McLean remembered that the staff was under pressure to "get the story first, but get it right." He wrote:

Reading the morning *Sentinel* was always an exercise in dread for Harvey Schwandner's reporters. All but the newest of us had some beat or area of responsibility—politics, medicine, farm, labor, etc. If the *Sentinel* carried some story in your area that in any possible way could have been sniffed out and run first in the *Journal*, you heard from Harvey.

One third, maybe one quarter, of the calumny fell on the news source. The rest landed on the lazy, inept, non-caring reporter.

Some of us thought that this harked back to the Front Page days of extras and significant street sales and was a little overdone. The effort to coax or bully breaks out of news sources could have a price in objectivity. No one, including the news sources, doubted that the size and tone of a story could vary significantly with which publication had it first.

Sometimes Harvey's outbursts seemed out of proportion to the event that triggered them. One instance of this occurred on a Saturday afternoon, when most of us were writing "think pieces" for the Sunday paper, where we usually had more space than in a daily edition. Here is what I saw happen:

For a while, my assistant on the political run was a reporter—younger than I—who had come to the *Journal* from a paper in Illinois. He had worked for a couple of months on the state desk and then was assigned as my assistant in covering politics after Robert Fleming, the other political reporter, left to join the Chicago bureau of *Newsweek.* This reporter had talent, but he had even more ambition; he may have been among the first of the new generation of reporters who were bolder than some of us because they were too young to have experienced the Depression.

On many Saturdays, depending on the political calendar, I would write what we called a "dope story." In such stories, you might look over the coming political season and speculate on what line the political parties might take, who might be looming as a dark horse candidate for something, and what the prospects might be for change in the Wisconsin political scene. What you needed to write such stories successfully—besides a good imagination—was some knowledge of Wisconsin history; familiarity with past and current rivalries, ambitions and alliances between politicians in both parties, and good contacts in both parties from whom you could extract confidential information and upon whom you could test your theories.

My assistant had a lively imagination, but he lacked the rest of these requirements. He had been in Wisconsin only a few months; he didn't have the background, and he didn't know enough people. But on this particular Saturday, without telling me, he produced a Sunday "dope story," put it on the city desk at Harvey Schwandner's left hand, then slipped back to his desk to watch the reaction. I think he expected to be commended for showing initiative. He hadn't been assigned to write that story. I watched, too. Harvey read some of it and and started to fidget. His face turned red. Two or three times he got up from his chair as if to head back to our side of the newsroom, but thought better of it and continued reading. Finally he finished it. He walked over to the writer's desk. Without saying a word, he took that long story and tore it end to end, then doubled it over and tore it crosswise until it was in tiny scraps. Then, using both hands, he threw the whole mess into the waste basket, dusted off his palms and walked back to the city desk.

The reporter had a temper, too. His face flushed, but he was too stunned to do anything for a few minutes. Finally, he walked over to the city desk and addressed Harvey.

"What's the matter?" he said. "Ed Bayley writes that kind of story every week."

"You're not Ed Bayley," Harvey snapped.

Fred L. Tonne, a longtime *Journal* photographer, emerged bewildered from an encounter with Harvey:

Photographers traditionally were not expected to "make words." I was not satisfied with this condition. the *Journal* sent me to Viet Nam in 1965, but nobody told me what to do there. I shot pictures, of course. But I also decided to write some stories to go with them. About 12 long stories and picture pages resulted, later syndicated by the ROP Color Service with some commercial success.

After I returned home and my pictures and stories had been published, I was leaving the office one day by chance with Harvey. He smiled wryly and said: "Think you're a reporter now with that Viet Nam stuff? Well, I read 'em!" That was all.

Avery Wittenberger reported this incident:

I attributed to Harvey's quizzical sense of humor an assignment he gave me while he was on the desk. Ordinarily, my reporting was confined to the county run, the courts or some phases of education. I had never been on the police run. One morning when I arrived at work there was a note that I was to cover a murder up in the Richfield area. The victim's name was Alvin Wittenberger. I think that the only reason that I got that assignment was that Harvey assumed that the man was a relative of mine and that Wittenberger ought to cover the demise of a Wittenberger.

As it turned out, the fellow was a distant cousin whom I had never met.

The late Mel Kishner, a *Journal* artist, who considered himself a personal friend of Harvey's, reported this unsettling brush:

> I had many encounters with Harvey's sharp wit, but the one I recall most vividly was when I submitted a sketch he ordered. He took one look at it and said, "If I was as bad with words as you are with a pen, I'd be working for the *Brookfield Shopping News* instead of the *Milwaukee Journal*."
>
> That comment really shook me and I asked what he would suggest that I do with the drawing. I was about to tear it up when he grabbed it back and said with that look we all knew so well, "Not a damned thing. It's great as it is." I never knew when he was needling me and when he wasn't.

In 1948, Harvey wrote a profile of Richard S. Davis, everyone's favorite reporter, for *Once A Year*, the Milwaukee Press Club's annual magazine. It is a wonderful piece and is reprinted at the end of this book. The following excerpt in which Harvey describes Dick Davis at work tells as much about Harvey as about Dick. It is what he wanted every one of his reporters to be.

> Much of the time the Davis approach to a story is emotional. It is this quality which makes him a great reporter, one of the greatest in the country. He can, however, dig facts with the best of diggers, especially when he is mad. Indeed, Davis is a journalistic triple threat—he can write marvelous feature stories, he can read copy and write headlines, and he can write a straight story. The latter, however, frequently proves a difficult chore for him. He just can't help being Dick Davis . . .
>
> His desk is a mess. Piled high are books, magazines, concert programs, notes from old assignments,

newspapers, letters from admirers, letters from guys who speak frankly of assaulting him, clippings—all these and more. But the Davis mind is neat, sharp, orderly. When he sits down to write a story, he is all concentration. Like a surgeon with a scapel, Davis works neatly with his typewriter. He hunches over the machine, punching expertly but slowly. His copy is a delight to copy readers. Seldom is there so much as a comma out of place. He thinks ahead. He knows exactly what he is going to say in the next paragraph. He is a precision writing instrument. He slaves at his work, struggling, searching, probing for the right word, the delicate phrase, the right ending. The Davis stuff is remarkable because he is willing to sweat like a butcher over it.

Harvey wanted all of us to sweat like butchers.

Chapter Two

ENTERPRISE

Reporters are inspired to do their best work by editors who are visibly excited by good stories that result from special enterprise.

Harvey had been a superb reporter and a deft writer before he became an editor. A well-handled story excited him. You knew it even though he was sparing with praise.

Hale Champion made this observation:

> What distinguished him from all the other city editors in my life was his view of what was news and how to shape a collection of chaotic details into a coherent story that ordered and identified what had happened. Most city editors live and die with stereotypes of what is and what isn't a story. Harvey loved—maybe liked is a better word in his case—the process of turning a non-story or a routine report into real news with a vivid detail, a further inquiry or even the opening of an unanswered, perhaps unanswerable, question.

Harvey would take risks to get a good story first, as John McLean reported:

> One of the biggest stories on my education beat in the early 1950s was the merger of the University of Wisconsin with the ten or so state colleges to form

11

the present state-wide university system. The most newsworthy appointment the university regents would have to make would be the head of the consolidated Milwaukee branch. It combined the existing university extension with a large state college.

The university regents would make the appointment at an afternoon meeting in Madison. The meeting would fall on *Sentinel* time, giving that paper the break on a big story. Ed Bayley heard that the regents had polled themselves in advance and were pretty well decided to name Dr. J. Martin Klotsche, president of the state college at Milwaukee. There was logic to the Klotsche appointment, but it was not a foregone conclusion. Klotsche, who had his own television show, was precocious and brash in the eyes of some old-line educators and had been positioned against the Madison leadership in some of the merger negotiations.

Harvey told me to go after the story; to get the Klotsche appointment into the *Journal* before the regents made it.

I didn't have good sources among the regents; they were regularly covered by the *Journal*'s Madison bureau. I began calling them one at a time. I told each that we understood that Klotsche was to get the appointment and waited for a confirming response.

The first two caught on to what I was doing and played innocent. The third, however, said, "Hey, that wasn't supposed to get out!" I got a kind of quiet confirmation from another regent and turned in the story: The *Journal* has learned that . . .

Harvey took one look at the story with its less than solid documentation. He could go with it and risk embarrassment like the *Chicago Tribune*'s famous "Dewey Defeats Truman" headline or he could read about the appointment in the *Sentinel*. He chose to play the story big, but he said to me: "John, go to Madison and cover the regents' meeting. If they don't go with Klotsche, you may not want to come back."

Fortunately, this was before the days of [President] Lyndon Johnson, who so hated leaks that he canceled appointments if they leaked before he could announce them officially. The regents were unhappy with the leak, but Joe Klotsche went on to a long and distinguished career as the first head of the University of Wisconsin-Milwaukee.

Pomfret's story of a "scoop" that blew up illustrates Harvey's willingness to take chances and his respect for enterprise even when it turned out badly. He wrote:

> The longest running big story that I covered during my eight years as the *Journal's* labor reporter was the United Automobile Workers' Union strike against the Kohler Company at Kohler, Wisconsin, a company town just outside Sheboygan. The strike went on for years, dividing the community, creating great bitterness and inflicting economic hardship.
>
> Late one day I got a tip from a union source that Emil Mazey, the UAW's secretary-treasurer and the senior union official in charge of the strike, was coming the next day from union headquarters in Detroit to speak at a meeting of the Kohler strikers in Sheboygan. My hunch was that Mazey was going to ask the members to vote to end the strike and offer to go back to work. The company had been hiring replacements. The union strategy, I suspected, was to try to win its unfair labor practices case against the company before the National Labor Relations Board, but in case that failed, to preserve as many jobs as possible for union loyalists by ending the strike.
>
> I knew Mazey well and the next morning I managed to get a call through to him at the UAW's headquarters in Detroit. After much hemming and hawing he confirmed my hunch, but strictly not for attribution to him. My problem was that I couldn't wait for the union meeting that afternoon because my deadline would have been long past and the *Sentinel*

would have beaten me on an important story. So I wrote a story predicting the end of the strike. Then I hopped into my car to drive to Sheboygan to cover the union meeting.

The union barred reporters from the meeting. It ran on and on into the afternoon. Meanwhile, the *Journal*, with my story predicting the end of the strike prominently displayed, was being distributed by the thousands all over the state. Finally the meeting broke up. A UAW publicist walked over to brief waiting reporters. Strictly routine, he said. Mazey had brought the members up to date, had answered their questions and the members had given the union a unanimous vote of confidence. What about the *Journal*'s story ending the strike? a reporter asked. Nothing to it, said the UAW man.

As the group broke up, one of Mazey's aides sidled over to me. "Emil is over at the hotel in the bar," he said. "He'd like to see you."

"I sure as hell want to see him," I said.

I found him sitting in a booth sipping a soft drink. "Interesting story in today's *Journal*," he said, grinning, as I sat down across from him.

"What happened?" I asked.

Mazey again insisted that I not attribute anything to him, then said: "I flew over here this morning with the union lawyer. We went through it all again. It was the first time I realized that to get the people back to work, we had to capitulate completely. It had to be unconditional surrender. I just couldn't do it."

When I walked into the office the next morning, the egg on my face felt like it had hardened and was going to stick there forever. I went over to Schwandner to explain as best I could what had happened. To my surprise, he didn't blow up. He actually smiled.

"Don't worry about it," he said. "Every good reporter has had stories that are still exclusives. Including me."

Jim Spaulding told two stories that illustrate Harvey's ability to inspire his reporters. He wrote:

> What excited and elated Harvey was anything special about reporting or writing. He liked to challenge his people. One morning at 11:45 he turned to me (on rewrite) and said, "Take Bergo on [extension] one and give me a funny piece." Jesus. Well, a judge in Waukesha County Circuit Court had just ruled against a plaintiff who had accused someone of causing an automobile accident by allowing a horse to run loose and cause a car to go off the road—something like that. The judge said the plaintiff hadn't proved there really was a horse. My lead was: "For want of a horse a suit was lost . . ." Harvey thought that was terrific. He and I grew up with something of the same background. Today a lot of readers wouldn't get the point.
>
> Another such incident that delighted Harvey concerned the Hindu medical faker, Dinsha Pustangi Ghadiali, who had just been released from the federal court's supervision. He was back in Milwaukee to announce to his followers his plans for his Spectrochrome Movement. The Spectrochrome was a fancy box with colored lights that was supposed to cure all kinds of diseases, including cancer, and among the many believers was Dan Hoan, the former mayor of Milwaukee. The event was to be at the Auditorium, and only card-carrying members of the movement were going to be admitted. I was on rewrite that day, too. Harvey was beside himself, trying to think of how to get a reporter into the meeting. I think I'm the one who suggested the solution. I covered a lot of Auditorium meetings and had noticed the presence of boxes from exhibitors who were arriving or leaving. Why not move a box over there and hide under it? Which is what we did, and when it worked (I was assigned to this, of course) Harvey could hardly

contain himself. That the *Sentinel* had been skunked was especially pleasing.

Jim's overly modest account of this feat omitted some interesting details. He neglected to say that he put on his World War II army uniform because some military group had just had a convention at the Auditorium. If detected, he could pretend to have been one of them, left over. He took a bottle of sherry along to further this illusion. He was nailed into the box, which had a peephole, and carried over there by *Journal* janitors. As it turned out, everything went according to plan.

At the time, Liz Wing thought one of her experiences with Harvey smacked more of sexism than of enterprise, but now . . . but let her tell it:

> After only a few weeks on the job, Harvey called me over to his desk one afternoon. "Can you swim?" he asked. "Yes," I said, adding proudly, "I'm a life-guard. Why do you ask?" He handed me a press release, telling me to read it and then we'd talk. It was about a featured act in a variey show opening that night. It claimed that a team of eight female swimmers would make umpteen complete costume changes under water in full view of the audience, each in only sixty seconds.
>
> "I want you down in the tank to check out the truth of their claim," Harvey said. I protested that I didn't have a swimming suit at the moment, that I emphatically didn't want to do it. "You're a reporter now," he said. "If you want to continue to be a reporter, you'll find a swimming suit and be at the show at 6:30 tonight."
>
> I was there, having borrowed a suit from my roommate. Each time the swimmers dived under and changed, I dived under and watched.
>
> After the show, just as I was deciding I could survive the experience with some dignity intact, a *Journal* photographer showed up. "All right, girls, four of

you on the right side of Liz and four on the left," he ordered. I said hey wait a minute, I didn't want any photo. He told me that Harvey had said to get a picture no matter what I said and he thought I'd better cooperate. So I did.

The next morning Harvey told me to write the story for the early edition. By that time, I was so mortified that I couldn't write a word. After badgering me to hurry up, Harvey saw that the writer's block was serious and sent Jim Spaulding over to interview me and write an "as told to" account. The photo and the story ran prominently that day.

On the face of it, this story demonstrates rank sexism. But when I think back, I remember that about ten days before Jim Spaulding had sneaked into a quack medicine show and had come up with a terrific story. Did Harvey see the swimmers' underwater change press release as just another opportunity for some investigative reporting? That may be an overly generous interpretation, but I don't think he meant to humiliate me and was genuinely sorry when I got upset.

Robert J. Doyle's story goes back to the days when Harvey was a rewriteman, himself. Bob intended it to illustrate Harvey's talent as a writer, but it also tells something about his ability to inspire reporters. He loved stories that showed up phonies. Doyle wrote:

I was in the office for a few weeks after eighteen months in the Southwest Pacific and six months in Europe as the *Journal*'s war correspondent, primarily looking for stories about Wisconsin servicemen. In January, 1945, while waiting for arrangements for me to be assigned to the Navy in the Pacific, I worked in the Milwaukee office.

Unfortunately for "Capt. James Saunders" I was sent to cover his talk to the Tymo Club at the Medford Hotel. In New Guinea, in September, 1943, I had been in the area described by the speaker as the scene of one of his exploits as a paratrooper.

I came back to the office and told whoever was on the city desk—maybe Arv Schaleben—that the guy was a phony. In any case, it was quickly decided that this was a story that required a real reporter and it was wisely assigned to Harvey, who was on rewrite, while I did more checking with army authorities and police.

Doyle said he loved Harvey's lead. It was:

A phony "paratroop captain" was unmasked Thursday afternoon by Robert J. Doyle, the *Journal*'s war correspondent, after the "captain" had sliced a huge ring of war combat baloney before the Tymo club at noon Thursday at the Medford hotel.

The story had no by-line.

Bob Dishon's story happened two years after the acquisition of the *Sentinel* by the Journal Company and Schwandner's appointment as *Sentinel* executive editor. It contains elements of inspiration and also makes the point that Schwandner could be just as fiercely competitive as the editor of the *Sentinel* as he had been as city editor of the *Journal*.

Bob's story concerns the release of a two-year study of Milwaukee's community renewal program—a 25-year program for replacing blight with new housing. Bill Manly, covering urban affairs for the *Journal*, had arranged with Mayor Henry Maier for release of the report at 10 a.m. on a Saturday, in time for the Sunday *Journal*. Reporters were offered the report two weeks in advance in exchange for their pledge to observe the official release date. The deal was made to give the *Journal* plenty of time to prepare a special section based on the report. Since the *Sentinel* no longer published a Sunday paper, it was going to be skunked on a big story.

Dishon, covering urban affairs for the *Sentinel*, declined to accept an advance copy of the report under the conditions laid down. Dishon never has disclosed how he did it, but on the Thursday before the fateful Saturday he got a copy of the report. He told Harvey of his coup. Harvey, according to Dishon, "went off the Richter scale."

Harvey and Dishon decided to publish the story on Saturday. Dishon finished writing the main article and two side stories on Friday afternoon.

His account continues:

> From Harvey on down the smiles in the newsroom were widespread. But Harvey was doing more than smiling. After the proofs had all been assembled, he decided to hold the whole thing out of the first edition. He had two things in mind—he wanted to be the first paper to publish the report, but he also wanted to create the most severe impact on the *Journal* for the trick they tried to pull on the *Sentinel*. If he had been in the *Journal*'s position, he would have done the same thing that they did, but he was pretty mad about the deal they had made with the mayor.
>
> He wanted the sharpest slap at the *Journal*. If the articles had gone into the first edition, the news would have been all over the evening radio and television news and the *Journal* would know the *Sentinel* had it. As it happened, the first time the *Journal* knew about it was when Harry Hill, the *Journal*'s assistant city editor, got to his desk at 6 a.m. Saturday. A short time later, he was phoning Manly and telling him to get to the office early and write a Saturday article because the story was all over the *Sentinel*. Manly was so busy writing the Saturday piece that he wasn't able to attend the press conference he had helped set up.

I remember the next story—my own—because Harvey liked it so much. It was also one of the infrequent instances where something tangible resulted because of a newspaper story. Here is what happened:

> I was the chief political reporter for the *Journal* at the time, but before that, I had been the city hall reporter. One day when political news was slow I was sent to cover the city hall on the regular city hall reporter's day off.
>
> It was a Thursday. That was always the city hall reporter's day off because little happened on Thursdays. The only committee that met on that day was the license committee, which issued licenses for taverns, liquor stores and bartenders, routine stuff that seldom produced news. This time, however, someone I knew appeared before the committee.
>
> Not only did I know him, but almost everyone in the *Journal*'s news and editorial departments knew him. He was Joe Wong, proprietor of La Joy, our favorite Chinese restaurant, which had started as a hole-in-the-wall near the paper, then moved out to a grander location. Joe had remodeled the building to make it a first-class restaurant.
>
> He was an applicant for a license to serve cocktails at the new place.
>
> He was represented by a lawyer, which was unusual, because applicants for liquor licenses seldom employed attorneys unless the applicant had a criminal record or something else that might have disqualified him. Joe Wong's background was spotless; he was a University of Wisconsin engineering graduate, active in civic affairs and highly respected in the community.
>
> And the attorney wasn't just any attorney. He was Milwaukee's best known criminal attorney, the kind of attorney who regularly appeared for the members of whatever organized crime there was in Milwaukee. What was Joe doing with that guy for his attorney? I wondered.

So I started taking notes, and I learned that this charade had been going on for six months, with a decision postponed over and over for no clear reason. There was a fixed number of liquor licenses in Milwaukee, and anyone who wanted to obtain one had to buy it from someone else. They cost from $10,000 to $25,000 at that time. Joe had complied with all the requirements; he had bought out the license of a skid row tavern. As a rule, the committee acted promptly and enthusiastically on this kind of transfer—the replacement of a license for a rundown bar with one for a respectable restaurant.

It became obvious to me that they were playing games with Joe, and I suspected that the lawyer was bleeding Joe for money to pay off the aldermen on the committee. I couldn't write that because I couldn't prove it, but I could say what was going on and let people draw their own conclusions.

As the hearing ended with yet another postponement, the lawyer came over to me. "You aren't going to write anything about this, are you?" he asked. I said I certainly was going to write about it.

The lawyer said that I should realize that if I wrote anything about it, Joe would never get his liquor license. I said I didn't believe that.

The lawyer asked if $75 would change my mind. Get out of here, I said. I was angry. *Journal* reporters did not take bribes.

Back at the office, I told Harvey, a longtime patron of La Joy, what I had and what the lawyer had done. Harvey put on his steely look and his face flushed.

"Take all the space you want," he said. "It's going on page one. "

It did, along with a page one editorial written by John Reddin, another Wong customer. The story and editorial appeared in Friday's paper. On Monday the license committee called a special meeting and, without discussion, granted the license.

Chapter Three

SUPPORT

If a newspaper is to aspire to excellence, its editors must do more than applaud reportorial enterprise. They must also back their reporters in the face of pressure from both outside and inside the paper.

The news business is stressful. Pressures are great. Reporters deal with hostile sources, with officials who are trying to conceal misdeeds, with politicians who lie and with business people who try to suppress negative stories. When editors of the paper back up their reporters against outside pressures, morale is high. When they fail to do so, morale, loyalty and performance languish.

I can think of no instance in which Harvey failed to back up a reporter, nor did anyone who responded to this project suggest such a failure. Enough correspondents cited examples of his support to make clear that he gave it instinctively.

In my view, this unwavering support and his enthusiasm for enterprise were Harvey's most important contributions to the success of the *Milwaukee Journal*.

"Harvey backed up his reporters in every case where it was at all possible to do so," said Rick Wing. He continued:

> When I covered city hall, many times aldermen
> and once in a while administrators wrote, called, or

came in to the *Journal* to say that I had mistreated them in one way or another. Sometimes Harvey had me talk to the complainant alone; sometimes he was present. But in every case, Harvey backed me up as his reporter, even though upon occasion (in the Zeidler-McGuire mayoral campaign, for example) there was a lot of "moneyed" pressure on Harvey.

The same was true when I was assigned to cover Joe McCarthy out in the state. McCarthy was campaigning, but the principal speaker was the American businessman, Robert Vogeler, a former captive of the Hungarians. The auditorium was packed. The speakers were late. I wrote that a large part of the audience "sat on their hands" for Joe, and more so for Vogeler. Some Republican woman wrote [Wallace] Lomoe saying that my story was wrong, that everyone had applauded both Joe and Vogeler. Lomoe called me in, and Harvey, too. I explained where I had been standing, how I had both heard and seen Joe's reception. Lomoe was noncommittal. Harvey backed me up 100 percent.

Hale Champion told a story that showed Harvey's readiness to back up a reporter and which also carried a message that, if you were dealing with Harvey Schwandner, it might not be wise to demand too much.

My best personal experience was the day after I had written a controversial story about aldermen who had accepted electric blankets from the city's electric utility. The story was written as humor disguised as sorrow rather than in terms of accusation and anger.

The pleasure of writing the story that way was sufficiently distracting so that I made a small error of fact, but one that only one of the aldermen or I might have caught. When the story appeared, I realized that I would have to beat the aldermen to the correction, but we ran a dead heat in getting to Harvey. Fortunately, their spokesman brought a lot of untrue complaints to the discussion as well, and I brought some damning new information about other gifts that had surfaced as a result of the first story.

Harvey sat like Solomon and listened to it all, then assured the complainant that the admitted mistake would be corrected on the front page (where the first story had been) the next day.

When we were alone, Harvey turned to me without a word of recrimination and said, "You'll have to write a full correction. It should be in the second or third paragraph of the second day story with all the new information in it. And don't forget to put back in everything from the original story that wasn't a mistake."

It was a pleasure to do business with a man who thought that everybody, not just reporters, should pay for their mistakes.

John Pomfret had two such experiences in his first year at the *Journal*:

I had been at the *Journal* for just a couple of weeks when I was given a routine handout from one of the big department stores to rewrite. I called the store's public relations office for verification and for additional information. The PR man said he wasn't going to answer any questions, that he expected the handout to be printed verbatim, and that he would like to remind me that his store was one of our biggest advertisers.

This was my first brush with an advertiser throwing his weight around and I went to Schwandner for instructions. As I told him what had happened, his face turned an angry red.

"You call that sonofabitch back," he said, "and tell him that, if he doesn't answer your questions, we'll never print a release from him again."

Before elections, the *Journal* published a tabloid with biographies of the candidates. Each reporter was given 10 or so of these to write. They followed a uniform format: age, occupation, education, political history, if any, etc.—the bare bones. We consulted the clips and interviewed the candidates to get the information. Pomfret recalled:

> I was dealing with candidates in the primary for the state assembly. One of them seemed to have difficulty remembering the year in which he had graduated from college. The deadline was approaching, so instead of waiting for the candidate to get back to me, I called the college. It turned out that he hadn't attended, let alone graduated. I began to check out everything he had told me. Most of it was untrue or exaggerated. I asked Schwandner what he wanted me to do.
>
> "Get him in here," he said.
>
> The candidate appeared the next afternoon. Schwandner walked up to him and, ignoring a proffered handshake, said: "There's a law in Wisconsin that makes it a crime to lie to a newspaper reporter. If you don't level with Pomfret here, we are going to use it on you." He wheeled abruptly and stalked away.
>
> We ran the candidate's biography, reporting what he first told me and what the facts were. The voters did not nominate him.

Sometimes, the pressure came through the business office when angry advertisers complained. Rick Wing tells of such an incident involving Liz Wing:

> Liz covered the "fur fashion show" at the State Fair. The handouts implied that the furs shown were mink, but Liz, after the show, went up and looked closely at the labels. All the coats were "mink-like" rabbit or squirrel, not one real mink. She wrote the story that way. The fur people went to Don Abert, the *Journal*'s business manager, and bitched. Abert went to Harvey. Harvey asked Liz if she had her notes. She did. She showed them to him. That ended it. Once again, Harvey backed up a neophyte as he backed up an experienced reporter.

Chapter Four

ACCURACY

Harvey loathed inaccuracy. The largest number of the stories contributed to this project deal with his struggle to put out a paper free of errors.

Most of the mistakes were committed by new reporters, some without previous newspaper experience. The largest number of the errors that surfaced were in obituaries. The *Journal* put new reporters on obits until they proved they could get them right, after which they got more challenging assignments.

Experience had taught that a mistake in an obit brought an angry phone call to the city desk faster than a mistake anywhere else in the paper. In those days of cheap newsprint and voluminous advertising, the *Journal* ran the obit of anyone whose survivors wanted one. The obit was going to be carefully preserved in the family archive and it had better be right. The eagle-eyed survivors were the best backup possible for a city editor who was fanatical about accuracy.

When Harvey questioned something in a story, he sent the copy back to the reporter with "Ask Harvey, pls" in his precise handwriting at the top. Some respondents remember the line as "See Harvey, pls" and it is likely that he used the two phrases interchangeably. The best tangible evidence is a large rubber stamp presented to the city editor by

Arthur Ochs (Punch) Sulzberger, chairman of the New York Times Company, who was a *Journal* obit writer in 1954. It says, "Ask Harvey, pls."

Sulzberger, called "Art" by most of his *Journal* colleagues, had been sent to the *Journal* by his father, Arthur Hays Sulzberger, publisher of the *New York Times,* to learn the craft of reporting. During most of his 10 months covering city news, Sulzberger wrote obits. His transfer to the state desk brought more varied duties. One of his encounters with Harvey was recounted by Alicia Armstrong:

> After writing an obit, Punch received a "See Harvey, pls" note, and he didn't immediately know why. He stood awkwardly at Harvey's desk for a time, and then it dawned on him that he had probably misspelled the word "mausoleum."
>
> "Oh," he said to Harvey, "you want to know how to spell mausoleum."
>
> "No," Harvey said. "I know how to spell mausoleum. I want you to know how to spell it. Then we'll have one thing in common."

Sulzberger wrote an appreciation of the *Journal* as a foreword to a history of the paper. It is reprinted at the end of this book.

Liz Wing, who joined the staff right out of Smith College, recalled her first day:

> Arriving for my first day of work, I was assigned a desk at the outer rim of the city room (just inside the railing and only a pace from the elevator). The only person within speaking distance was Punch.
>
> I sat alone, unneeded and growing anxious, reading first the previous day's, then that day's various editions. The morning went by. Finally, Harvey came over with a press release on a meeting some do-gooder group was to hold. He told me to check out the release by phone for accuracy, then write a couple of paragraphs about it. Punch, observing my anxiety,

was kind enough to offer to look over the story. He made a couple of suggestions for changes and I followed his advice.

Later, reviewing my story with me, Harvey asked why I'd phrased something the way I had. "Punch told me that was how I should do it," I said. Harvey said nothing, but the next morning my desk had been moved away from Punch's and next to that of Andy Galvin, who proved to be a lifesaver for me in my early weeks at the *Journal*.

Punch was a natural, modest person with a good sense of humor, popular with his fellow reporters. He was often dismayed by Harvey's criticism, but never lost his sense of perspective.

Laura Pilarski recounts that Punch posted on the bulletin board a copy of an article from some publication that described his *Journal* apprenticeship as "learning about policy." He added a note: "There will be a policy meeting of obit writers at 9 a.m. today."

Harvey liked that and chuckled over it for a long time, Laura said.

John McLean was one of Sulzberger's contemporaries who watched him struggle with obits. He said that Sulzberger knew that he was not a great reporter. "He had the education and the scope of interests, but he lacked accuracy in small details," John said. He continued:

Once at our house, Art and I and George Groh got to the third drink and Art said in a halting fashion, unusual for him, "Let me ask you a kind of personal question that has been bothering me. You don't have to answer if you don't want to."

"Go ahead," we said.

"Well, the other day I made a mistake in an obituary. I got the wrong day for the funeral. I guess some people complained. Harvey really lit into me. I've never been bawled out like that. My question is: Was

I getting some special treatment? Do you think my family told the *Journal* to be especially tough on me?"

"You don't have to worry," George told him. "You got standard treatment."

When Harvey died, Alicia Armstrong sent a copy of the *Journal*'s obituary to Punch. She quoted part of his reply:

I notice with great relief that the obit did not say that he died "suddenly." I remember having written that years ago and being summoned before Harvey and told that everyone dies suddenly—one minute you're alive and the next you're dead. In Milwaukee, people died unexpectedly . . . and I still can't spell mausoleum . . .I was pleased to read that his "after work humor" was delightful. At any rate, he was a great teacher and I owe him a lot.

From Tom Blinkhorn, I learned that it was possible to be demoted from writing obits. He reported:

Arv Schaleben hired me to work at the *Journal.* I had only a perfunctory interview with Harvey, although I had been warned well in advance by *Journal* contacts from Marquette University, where I had studied, about his proverbial temper. I soon was to experience it first hand.

Although I had been covering local politics, city hall and the federal building at the *Cincinnati Enquirer,* I was quickly given to understand that starting out young at the *Journal* meant (a) obits and (b) if you did well at that, you could cover the flag day parade at Waubeka. Jim Wieghart started about the same time, and he and I set out to try to figure out how to handle Harvey. Alicia Armstrong gave us a full briefing about the changing colors of his physiognomy and what each meant. Thus armed, we felt reasonably confident in being able to handle the situation. My confidence was strengthened further by the fact that I had endured George Carr, city editor at the *Enquirer,* who loved to scream across the city room at "college kids who don't know how to spell or write a simple declarative sentence."

Harvey was not a screamer but he sure as hell could pack a wallop. The first one came after two days on the job. I had turned in an obit about some character on the south side who had made a mark building bird houses. "See Harvey, pls" came back to me and I was soon in line waiting to see the great man. He gave me a cursory glance and then put me in my place with a phenomenal recollection of virtually every line in that stupid obit, including the address of the funeral home, which could not possibly have been correct, he insisted, and the date of the man's birth, which didn't jibe with another fact in the story.

"Go back and start over," he growled. Away I went.

On the basis of that performance, I was demoted to Cappy Dick, a reader contest. My job was to make sure the winners' names and addresses were correct. I had completed most of the work but one name in particular was giving me trouble.

I took the copy home with me on my day off—a Friday—not realizing that the task had to be completed in time to make the Sunday paper. Later that day, I received a phone call from Bill Radloff, Harvey's assistant.

"Harvey wants to see you right away, and bring the Cappy Dick information with you," he said.

I quickly made my way to Fourth and State [the *Journal*'s location], copy in hand. Harvey was pink, so I knew I was in trouble. He lectured me on the importance of Cappy Dick to *Journal* readers, why facts had to be checked and double checked and why I should never take important copy home with me. He gave me 15 minutes to finish the piece. I managed to get the last address and get it in to the master on time. He looked at it for 10 seconds, making sure the addresses were okay, and let it go.

Like Blinkhorn, Stanley Zuckerman came to the *Journal* with previous experience. But he, too, started out with obits, and learned how serious Harvey was about getting the facts right:

> My first encounter with Harvey, other than a general awareness of his beady-eyed presence as he insinuated himself silently about the newsroom, was the result of an early obit assignment. Harvey hadn't hired me. A professor at the University of Wisconsin had referred me to Paul Ringler, a *Journal* editorial writer, who passed me on to Harry Sonneborn and Arv Schaleben. I wasn't truly aware of the managerial hierarchy, nor of Harvey's role in the editorial process. Despite a couple of years' experience on a morning daily in Columbus, Georgia, and an MA from the University of Wisconsin, I was seated with the other "birdlings," as Dick Davis called us, in a corner of the newsroom reserved for the "necrologists," another Davis label. We learned *Journal* style by cranking out obituaries until we could be entrusted with coverage of weightier matters, such as the deliberations of the town of Mequon planning commission.
>
> I had been at the *Journal* only a week or so. I was racing to finish up work one evening before taking off for Madison. The drive took several hours, delayed by the separation of my muffler and tail pipe. I arrived in Madison to learn that I had been called repeatedly by Harvey, who wanted me to call back immediately. Since it was already past 10 p.m., there was no way to get him until morning. I slept uneasily, wondering what urgent assignment was in store for me. My quick mastery of the *Journal* stylebook had, I hoped, commended me to the Front Office.
>
> I called the *Journal* at 7 a.m. and found Harvey there. The conversation went something like this:
>
> "Harvey, this is Stan Zuckerman. I was told you had an urgent message for me, and I'm sorry I

couldn't get back to you until this morning. I arrived late last night. What can I do for you?"

"You can tell me how to spell Kleinman." (Or Kreitzman, or Kupperman—some good Milwaukee name certainly of a gentleman who had died the day before and whose obituary I had written.)

"You have it spelled two different ways in the obit," Harvey said, "one way in the lead and another way in the third paragraph."

"Good God, Harvey," I said, "I thought it was something major to have caused you to chase me all over the state. Anyone could have looked that up in the city directory."

"**YOU** could have," Harvey said, and hung up.

Liz Wing's roommate—on the receiving end in a case of mistaken identity—got a shock when she answered the phone early one morning on Liz's day off to be greeted by: "This is Harvey. Goddammit, didn't anyone ever teach you to spell Tucson?"

John Pomfret, too, learned about that cardinal sin of newspaper work—misspelling a name. He wrote:

> Schwandner was the master of the short, waspish, mortifying note. While still a probationer, I was assigned to cover a speech that he gave to a gathering of journalists at Marquette University. His only instruction to me was to keep the story short. I wrote a few paragraphs and dropped the copy on his desk. In a few minutes, a grinning copy boy brought it back. Schwandner had circled his own name and beside it had written: "Who he?" I had misspelled his name, omitting the final n.

The late Eugene Harrington recalled his days among the writers of obituaries:

> I started at the *Journal* in June, 1958, as a general assignment reporter under Harvey. My desk was across from those of Dick Davis, Alicia Armstrong and

Larry Osman, and next to that of Jim Wieghart, who had started about a month after I did. Since we were new, Jim and I often got the obits and, as you might know, Harvey not only demanded that we get the names, addresses and ages right, but the names of the morticians as well.

Jim had problems with spelling and when Harvey found he couldn't even spell "cemetery" right, he kept him on obits for days and days. I still remember how hard Harvey pushed him when he was angry and giving him a hard time. Jim told me that as he was starting for work one Saturday his little two-year-old daughter said, "Do you have to do obits from Harvey again, Daddy?"

Carl Eifert, too, remembers that Wieghart had particularly annoyed Harvey:

For a time I sat in a bank of desks directly across from Jim Wieghart, who sat next to the revered Dick Davis. Each morning we would go to our boxes and claim our assignment slips for the day. My dread was obits. Luckily, I caught no more than my share. Jim, however, being the outspoken guy he has continued to be, had risen high on Harvey's retribution list and his reaction to writing obits day after day was anything but acceptance.

Tom Blinkhorn told of another aspect of the Schwandner-Wieghart hostility:

Wieghart and I used to spend a lot of time in the cafeteria, and in the local bars, trading Harvey stories. Jim was determined to psych him out, even though he was constantly in Harvey's doghouse. One trick I particularly remember was Jim's handling of Harvey's nod. Harvey would seldom say hello (or anything else friendly) to new staff members. On occasion, however, he would nod. Jim's trick was to approach Harvey in the hallway, look him straight in the face from a distance, catch Harvey's eye, and just as Harvey was to give his nod, quickly turn away. It was one of Jim's ways of getting even.

Liz Wing had a subtler way of getting even with Harvey:

> I was always on obits, or so it seemed, though actually it was probably only three days out of five. It didn't take me long to realize that to get along with Harvey meant fighting back. Harvey had high blood pressure and (I've forgotten how I found this out) was anxious about his heart. My revenge consisted of watching for 45-year-old men who died of heart attacks. When I got one, I would bring it to Harvey, wearing an expression of great concern, and say: "Isn't this guy about your age?" He always laughed, and I would be relieved from obits for several days after that.

Stuart Hoyt, like some others, recalls that Harvey's tolerance of error was short-lived:

> I got whipped into shape by Harvey on my first day as a reporter. He reminded me fairly gently that Waukesha had no "u" at the end. But soon he was treating me as gruffly as anyone else. It got so that I enjoyed going to work only on his days off. I looked forward to his vacations as much as he did.
>
> One day when I was on obits, Harvey called me over to his desk. He told me that I had gotten the name of the funeral home wrong in an obit for a former Milwaukeean that had been phoned in from out in the state. My jaw dropped. The funeral home was in some dinky town I had never heard of. How would Harvey have known I had gotten it wrong? How would he have known what to change it to? Well, he ceremoniously corrected my copy and passed it on. He wasn't nasty. He was even pleasant as he excused me. I went back to my desk in a daze, with enhanced

respect for this city editor who seemed to know EVERYTHING. It wasn't until later that I found out that the little town—Brillion—was where Harvey came from! He never let on to me that he had been pulling my leg.

Mike Harris, who spent a year or two at the *Journal* before moving on to New Orleans and eventually the *San Francisco Chronicle,* said that both Harvey and Arv Schaleben were great teachers, and that he owed a lot to each of them. He wrote:

> I recall only one time when I saw Harvey let his anger show and I'm pleased to say I was not the target. You recall, I'm sure, that we used to paste our stories together before turning them in. I remember that a young woman, new on the staff, wrote two obits and then erred by pasting the wrong second page on both. When Harvey pointed out what she had done wrong, she burst out laughing. That was her second mistake. She wasn't around much longer.

That story illustrates what I see as the trigger for Harvey's fiercest outbursts. One error, even two, he could forgive, but what he could not tolerate was a reporter who didn't care about errors, who didn't think an error was serious. I saw an example of this one morning in 1947 from a seat at the rewrite desk:

> Kenny Smith was on police rewrite that day. He was a talented writer, good at feature stories, and he knew he was good. He was younger than most of us, and he had no family to support, and he was brash.
> That morning he was taking a story from an upstate correspondent about an automobile accident in the Fox River valley, 100 miles north of Milwaukee. The story was being handled by the city desk, rather than the state desk, because the people involved were from Milwaukee.

> The police rewriteman sat a few feet to the right
> and a few feet back of the city editor. Kenny handed
> Harvey the first take on the story. The dateline was
> Fond du Lac.
> "I thought this accident was in Oshkosh,"
> Schwandner said.
> "Oshkosh, Fond du Lac, what's the difference?"
> Smith muttered.
> Harvey jumped up, his face red. He was so angry
> he was spluttering.
> "Get out! Get out! You're fired!" he yelled. He
> pushed Smith across the city room, rang for the ele-
> vator and pushed him in. That was the last we saw
> of Kenny Smith.

"He made no allowances for carelessness," said Harry
Sonneborn, who worked for Harvey at both Milwaukee
newspapers. He continued:

> He expected a reporter, after writing a story, to go
> over it with care, correct typos, and be sure that
> names and addresses and facts were right.
> Once I ran into a young man who had started as
> a night police reporter, a promising fellow who had
> quit after a few months. A night police reporter wrote
> his stories and memos toward the end of his shift and
> left them to be read first thing in the morning by the
> city editor. Then he would turn in and sleep until early
> afternoon, or try to.
> "Why did you quit?" I asked him.
> "I got tired of being waked up after a half hour of
> sleep by Harvey demanding to know how to spell the
> word 'the'," he said.
> That was Harvey, reminding the young cub in a
> brutal way that he had to correct every typo.

Marion Wilhelm, who went from the *Journal* to a career
as a foreign correspondent, also remembered this kind of
discipline:

> Harvey Schwandner, who hired me from the *City News Bureau* of Chicago, gave me my basic training in reporting. Ouch! Harvey's was not the rough language of the police captains and rewrite men I had heard in the summer of 1947 as a police reporter for the *City News* at the Chicago Avenue police station. But, the volume and precision of his reactions to a naive 22-year-old from a small town in northern Wisconsin gave me hope that "if" I ever learned to spell, "if" I ever learned to speak up, and "if" I ever learned to get the facts straight, I "might" become a *Journal* reporter.

Even experienced reporters were taught lessons that lingered in the mind. Rod Van Every, who later became the *Journal*'s city editor, was one. He recalled this painful episode:

> Once, on police rewrite, I placed a court in the wrong building, either the courthouse or Safety Building, I can't remember. Harvey did not like that. He ordered me to go to both buildings and get acquainted with them. I returned six months later after being assigned to the police beat, the most miserable six months of my life.

Bill Hibbard said that Harvey was a "stickler for accuracy." What Bill did to cope with this was to write in his *Journal* style book the spellings of names and places in Milwaukee that had been brought "forcefully to my attention" by Harvey—such things and places as Misericordia hospital, St. Josaphat's basilica, Michigan St. (not Ave., as in Chicago).

"That list was pasted in succeeding style books until I retired 38 years later," Hibbard said.

Even the photographers sometimes ran into trouble with Harvey. In 1947 George (Sam) Koshollek was new to the staff and worked in the photographic lab. He wrote:

I wanted to be published, so I spent my spare time looking for pictures the paper might use. I turned in some photos of people taking a romp in the surf of Lake Michigan in late October. The next day I went to the picture desk to see if my photo was going to be used. While I was there, this little short guy came over from the city desk and wanted to know what idiot had turned in a weather picture without giving the complete addresses of the people. I never made that mistake again in 37 years on the *Journal*.

"It was Harvey Schwandner's belief," said John McLean, "and a deeply held tenet at the *Milwaukee Journal*, that a reader who caught you not knowing whether Vliet was a street or an avenue was not going to believe you when you wrote about Joe McCarthy or the United Nations."

Bob Wills, who worked under Harvey at the *Journal* and later succeeded him as editor of the *Sentinel*, spoke at the funeral service for Harvey in 1988. He described what happened when someone got a note saying "See Harvey, pls":

"Seeing Harvey" could be one of the great educational experiences of a young reporter's life. Sometimes Harvey played games. "There's a misspelled word (or name) on that piece of copy," he would say. "Find it." Sometimes he challenged a fact. "No parrot ever weighed eight pounds." The reporter was left to find out who was right.

The directive was issued calmly but firmly. It was not an invitation to banter with the boss. Sometimes, if the issue or the charges in a story were serious, he'd be stern but friendly. You knew he was on your side because he discussed vulnerability and liability. And he came to your desk. At other times, he'd throw your copy on the desk and suggest with biting sarcasm that perhaps your future would be better assured if you switched to selling insurance.

Behind all of this was an obsession for accuracy. It was a magnificent obsession. He instilled it in his staff, and left it as a legacy for generations to come.

"I didn't invent accuracy," he once said, "but I'm interested in it."

Chapter Five

PUNCTUALITY

Next to accuracy, Harvey was most passionate about punctuality. He was punctual himself. He left work every day at 3 p.m., even refusing to take phone calls from his wife if he was already on his way out.

He rose from his desk at the same time each day to go to the composing room to watch the city report being put to bed by the printers. On his way upstairs, he dropped into the men's room, always using the same urinal. Rod Van Every, a close observer of his habits, once posted a note above it. It said: "Harvey is mean to reporters."

Deadlines were sacred and so were starting times.

Several people contributed essentially the same story about Harvey's rages when reporters came late to work. I saw this happen to Bob Fleming. John McLean saw it happen to Neil McKay. But only one person told the story in first person, Jerry Kloss:

> Many, I am sure, have told of Harvey's gift for skinning a miscreant alive. The telltale sign of displeasure was the flush of red at the back of the neck, known variously among the cognoscenti as the Schwandnerometer, or Red Alert.
>
> "Red Alert!" someone would whisper on Stow Row, where the general assignment reporters sat. We'd keep an eye out to see who was getting the "Ask

Harvey, pls" note. If we were close enough, we could catch the ensuing one-way conversation, such as a snarled: "Are you going to leave that body mouldering at the Becker Funeral Home or do you plan to give it a decent burial?"

Sometimes his fury had to be given an immediate outlet—no waiting for an "Ask Harvey, pls" note. I was on the receiving end one memorable morning, when I arrived at work about two minutes late. As soon as I sat down, somebody whispered, "Red Alert!"

"Me?" I asked.

"Who else?"

I patted back a totally fake yawn and turned to see Harvey advancing on me, stiff-legged, as if his limbs were engorged with blood. He cricked his neck twice.

"Where the hell have you been, Kloss?"

"Harvey, I'm only two minutes late, maybe three!"

I'll never forget his next words, uttered in a cast-iron voice:

"How would you like to hang by your neck for two minutes?"

Over the last forty years, I've never thought of a good answer to that.

Other times, however, he could be unexpectedly forgiving over a more serious infraction. One time I was hours late getting to work after a major night on the town. All the way to work I was wondering what possible excuse I could come up with. Nothing came to mind, so I was set to face the music when I walked into the city room.

My desk then was located against a back wall on the east side of the city room. I tried to sidle over, keeping close to the wall, like a cornered rat. When I got to my desk, I hunched into my chair, as if keeping my head low would offer some kind of protection And . . .

NOTHING HAPPENED!

I threw furtive peeks at Harvey ever so often. The Prussian nape was normal. No "Ask Harvey" notes in the in-box, not even a glance in my direction from the City Desk. What was going on?

Then it happened. I took another peek at Harvey, and he turned and looked at me. Our eyes locked, and he broke into laughter. So did everybody else on rewrite, all of them in on the gag of watching me try to sneak in without being noticed. Why Harvey happened to let this go by I've never known and I never asked.

Harvey was particularly harsh with those whose tardiness or absenteeism was the consequence of strong drink. It wasn't that he minded drinking; he enjoyed it himself. But he expected you to get to work on time even if you were carousing until dawn, no matter how bad you felt.

Harvey did not socialize with the younger reporters off the job. It wasn't that he turned down invitations; he simply never invited us to his house and it never occurred to us to invite him to ours. An exception was a dinner given one evening in 1948 by William S. Fairfield, who had grown up in a posh neighborhood on the east side of Milwaukee and was socially confident. He was a summer intern at the *Journal* between his junior and senior years at Harvard University where he was managing editor of the *Crimson*. Bill's parents were out of the city and he invited the Schwandners and my wife and me over for dinner. I have never forgotten that night:

The senior Fairfields had an account at a meat market named Franks'—the best in town. Bill had ordered a beef rib roast—four or five ribs—for the occasion. He had not, however, asked for cooking directions. When we all arrived at the house at 7 p.m., we found that Bill had the drinks ready, but had made no plans for cooking the roast. The women soon set him straight and the roast went into the oven as soon as it could be made ready. But it was a long time before it was done.

Meanwhile, the gin flowed. Bill kept dispensing martinis and Harvey kept drinking them. "Just a squirt," he would say, accepting another refill. It was a long, fuzzy evening, but it was good-natured, and Harvey made it so.

It was about 2 a.m. when the party broke up. Harvey looked pointedly at Bill and me. "See you at seven," he said. We were there.

But poor J. Paul O'Brien, under similar circumstances, failed to appear on time one morning for police rewrite. Jerry Kloss saw it happen:

Harvey gave O'Brien half an hour to show up, then asked me (also on rewrite) to call him at home. I did that, got O'Brien's wife on the phone and relayed her message that poor old Paul was ailing something awful and simply couldn't make it in to work. Harvey nodded and told me to tell Mrs. O'Brien that he would appreciate it if Paul could struggle to the phone for a brief discussion about something. She said she'd try and a minute later Paul said, "Hello?" in as sick-sounding a voice as he could come up with. I nodded to Harvey and he picked up the phone.

"Paul," he said quietly, "you may not remember, but I was at the Press Club last night, too, and I probably had as many drinks as you had, if not more. But the difference is that I came to work this morning, no matter how bad I felt, but you, goddammit"—and here he started rising from his seat, to match the rise in his voice—"you DIDN'T! And I'm saying, if you don't get your ass down here in 20 minutes—no, make that 15 minutes—you can forget about coming back here PERIOD!" He slammed down the phone, tossed his shoulders like a rampaging bull and sat there, glancing at his watch.

So did I. Paul made it in 14 minutes, slinking in with his shirttails out. Oh, he looked pitiful. And I learned a great moral: When you drink with the boss-man, make damned sure that you don't come down with polio or quinsy or glanders the next morning.

Chapter Six

PERSONALITY

What was Harvey like? He was of middling height and slightly built. He had a face like a hatchet. His nose was long and thin and pointed. His lips were often pursed as he contemplated the crimes and misdemeanors of the reporters under his command.

He was quintessentially tidy: the carefully knotted tie, the crisply starched shirt, the sharply creased trousers, the well-polished shoes, the thinning brown hair always slicked back and neatly trimmed.

He worked coatless, shirtsleeves always rolled above his elbows to keep them out of the paper dust, pencil grit, ink and glue drippings that accumulated on editors' desks in the days before computers introduced hygiene into newsrooms.

David Wiggins remembered him this way:

> I'm not sure what a city editor was supposed to look like, but I know Harvey did not look like one. His voice was all wrong for it, as well as his personality. He made good, I believe, the same way Jim Taylor once scored a touchdown against Cleveland in a desperate moment. He simply willed himself into the end zone, disregarding the protoplasm in his way.

Jim Spaulding, to whom I sent a copy of Wiggins' letter, wrote:

> I think Dave Wiggins has a point. Schwandner was essentially colorless—sort of pale, undistinguished looking, medium height, medium everything except the exceptionally sharp reporter's mind and aggressiveness. Behind that colorless exterior, he was a real shark, which we all realized quickly.

Joe Shoquist said he had the good fortune not to have had to work for Harvey, but he worked on the telegraph desk when Harvey was city editor. They came to work at the same time, about 5 a.m. He said:

> The positions of our two desks were such that the telegraph editor sat with his back to the city desk about 20 feet away. I learned in a hurry to say nothing, not even good morning, to Schwandner. We sat at our respective desks and worked in silence—most of the time.
>
> On occasion, Harvey would throw a temper tantrum, all by himself. Usually, he would just swear. Sometimes he would shout. When he really got wound up, he would throw things.
>
> Once, I recall, he climaxed his tantrum by hurling his bell across the room. Sitting there with my back to him, I probably jumped in my chair but I never turned around and I never said a word. Harvey was not a man to cross at 5:30 a.m.
>
> Later in the morning, of course, when he felt he had the day's copy flow under control, he would relax and become civil. I rarely talked to him, though, unless I had to.

Rod Van Every observed some of this early morning behavior, too:

> He was in no mood for greetings or discussing the weather. Storm clouds seemed to float over his head. In sifting through the assignments made the afternoon before by the assistant city editor, he glowered, he slapped some memos hard on his desk, scribbled furi-

ously on them. I came to believe that Harvey hated his lot in life that forced him to roll out of bed so early, day after day after day.

If I had been making those assignments the previous afternoon, I'd sketch out a smiley face with the greeting—"Good morning, Harvey"—and slip it into the middle of the pile. This was designed to brighten his morning or to infuriate him; I can't remember which.

Rick Wing added to this description:

Harvey was sometimes amused by a person or a story. He had an enthusiastic but quiet little chuckle. When he laughed, it was as though he was swallowing his chuckle; he didn't want to be loud. I remember him sitting at his desk, reading copy, writing memos. When he got dressed up, as for a civic dinner, he looked neat and clean but he never looked like an executive. He looked like a guy from Brillion who was embarrassed to be among Milwaukee's elite.

Harry Sonneborn provided this portrait:

Harvey was a terror to young reporters but he had a fine sense of humor. Before he became assistant city editor, he had been the rewrite man who always was assigned the humorous feature of the day. He wrote with a light and sophisticated touch, and he knew just when to stop writing and let the events speak for themselves.

He enjoyed a good joke, and he laughed as heartily as anyone when humor was injected into an otherwise pontifical meeting. He liked to relate funny things that happened—usually to other people—but I never heard him tell a joke.

He often said he didn't like labels. But he applied labels freely himself when dealing with and describing people. So-and-so was a "talker." Another was "a politician," "a city room lawyer." Another was "a woman chaser." He would use the same descriptive word every time the subject came up and he would let it echo there, expecting you to know all the characteristics that the word implied. If we were discussing a certain reporter, Harvey might mention that the subject was a Jew. Harvey avoided any overt anti-Semitic words or actions, but he probably had a shade of prejudice. To him, a Jew had certain characteristics which he never spelled out, but he expected you to know what they were as well as he did.

In such conversations, I always reminded him that I was a Jew (my paternal grandparents were Jews, but my father had long rejected all organized religion). I don't think he believed me. He wouldn't say anything, but would give me that well known owlish stare.

Harvey didn't like off-color humor. He was a most proper person. The traditional proprieties were important to him and he wanted everyone to observe them.

We sent a reporter to Vietnam for a long stay and he came back with a collection of good, off-beat, unconventional stories about the unwritten side of the war. Harvey was totally disgusted with the man, because he had never once communicated with his wife at home. Harvey was not satisfied until the man committed a flagrant offense and was fired.

Was he stuffy? Some thought so, but he could let his hair down and toss dignity aside. He worked hard and few would argue that he was not an excellent city editor. He set high standards but he knew better than to expect everyone to meet them. There were people on the staff who could not do everything well, and Harvey made allowances for them.

Harvey was loyal—loyal not only to his paper and to his family, but to his oldest friends. They were not necessarily the outstanding newsmen of the kind Harvey was, but they went back a long way together, and that was enough for him.

He kept his own finances meticulously solvent and he thought people who had financial problems probably had serious flaws of character. Yet he was soft hearted about people who had problems which were not of their own making. He helped many people out of his own pocket and did not press for repayment unless prosperity was evident, in which case he expected to get his money back. The proprieties again.

I have seen tears in his eyes more than once when he was moved by the death of someone not especially close to him, and at least once when he was moved by a story about courage in the face of hardship.

Avery Wittenberger wrote:

Harvey was a bit eccentric, I always thought, but a good reporter, writer and editor. I particularly admired his succinct style of writing and wry sense of humor. He was not a guy you got to know easily. I often wondered if I ever really knew him. Carrying on a conversation with him was like trying to interview a hostile news source.

He was still a reporter when I came to the *Journal* in 1943. When I took over the courthouse run eight months later, I felt that he and I had one thing in common—he had covered the courts at one time, so he had been there himself.

He knew my beat and many of the people on it, and this provided us some rapport. He understood what I was trying to do. During his years as city editor, I received my share of "See Harvey" memos, but I can't recall that they ever threw the fear of God into me as they apparently did for some of the younger reporters.

I did have more than a passing acquaintance with Harvey, however, since we were neighbors and attended the same church during my early years at the *Journal.* Occasionally, Gordy Hecker, Harvey and I would team up to attend such functions as the infamous Press Club stag parties and the annual *Journal* Christmas parties. On such occasions

> I came to know that the quiet, sober Schwandner was capable of letting his hair down. Come Sunday mornings, though, as an usher and deacon at the Roosevelt Drive church he was the typical straight-laced Presbyterian.

In conversation and on a platform, Harvey tended to be short and sharp. John Pomfret found that out when he asked a silly question:

> I came to the *Journal* straight out of college, just a few weeks after my 21st birthday. I was still pondering the meaning of life. I blush to recall it, but one day over lunch in the cafeteria I asked Schwandner to tell me his personal philosophy. He looked at me in amazement and said, "There are good guys and there are sons of bitches" and returned to munching his sandwich.

Monica Bayley went to a dinner at the Milwaukee Press Club for Warren Beck, a Lawrence College English professor, novelist and an authority on the life and works of William Faulkner. She had majored in creative writing under Beck at Lawrence. Harvey, too, had taken courses from Beck when he was at Lawrence, and he thought highly of him.

Those at the dinner were Beck's former students. Harvey had been asked to introduce him, and he did, in a way.

"This is a man who needs no introduction," he said, and sat down.

Bob Wills tells about another short speech:

> Once the *Sentinel* played host to a visiting journalist who was swollen with her own importance. She couldn't handle the name "Schwandner." She referred repeatedly to Henry Schwinner, to whom she was grateful. Harvey listened with amusement while the rest of us suffered irritation. It came his turn to speak.

"My name's Henry Schwinner and I've just bought your dinner," he said, and sat down.

Jack Krueger contributed the transcript of a tape recording made in 1980 of remarks by Harvey on the subject of his presidency of the Milwaukee Press Club. He employs the same clipped style of speaking:

The years fly. When was I the Press Club president? Way back in 1945 and 1946. It began this way. I was working in the *Journal* city room. Arv Schaleben and Hap Gladfelter were staring at me. I wondered what scheme they were cooking up. Soon they walked over.

"We want you to run for president," Arv said. And so my service began.

The club was stumbling along on the 8th floor of the Jung Building on North Water Street. It was dead in the water. The manager was Bill Streich, a grouchy old German. He wanted to keep the club as quiet as possible. If a visitor pushed a magazine out of place, Bill would frown and quickly put it back in line.

A few of us began talking about getting a bar in the club to make money and to liven up the place. Streich opposed the idea. He wouldn't have it, he said. A vote was finally taken, and we won. There would be a bar. I visited Sol Abrams, a strong man at the Schlitz brewery. Abrams scowled at me. He lit his pipe. His black eyes pierced me. I told him about our plans to get a bar. Would he help? Well, he puffed for a while. Then he mellowed. He told me how to get a bar and how to set it up. We were on the way.

I trotted to the City Hall to get a license. I visited several companies that made bars and set them up. The bar was in my name until I put it in the club's name. I never wanted to be known as a saloonkeeper. The bar and lunch brought in our people. Bill Streich quit. Bless him. Now long gone.

Billy Pohl, our good friend for years, liked to have a drink at the club. He also liked shaking dice. I usually lost, but the sport made a pleasant thump, thump, thump.

I remember some of the famous people who visited the club. Bob Hope dropped in. So did Marshall Field of Chicago, and Edna Ferber, the writer.

I will always remember the worn food tables. They had been scrubbed over and over. Bless the presidents that followed me. They all did a fine job. The club deserves a healthy future.

Stuart Hoyt said that Harvey was at his "mellowest" on the Saturday night shift when most of the people on duty in the city room ate dinner at the George Diamond steak house in the old Republican Hotel.

"On such occasions rank was overlooked," he said, "and the lowliest new reporter was welcome to join in merry conversation with the loftiest of editors. Once back in the city room after dinner, one had to be on one's guard again, though not so much as during the week."

Jerry Kloss remembered some of Harvey's quirks, things he used to wonder about:

I admired Harvey's will power in stifling sneezes until he had removed his glasses, so as not to mist the lenses with the spray. Some mornings, when he had a bad cold, he'd spend half the time removing and putting on his glasses, but not once would he sneeze with his glasses on. A strange thing to remember about a man, but there it is.

I also remember a toast he used to utter before sipping a drink. While others would say "Here's how!" or "Down the hatch!" or "Cheers!" Harvey would look you in the eye and chant "To cubic inch displacement!" Why? I never asked.

Chapter Seven

POLITICS

Many of us have puzzled over Harvey's political convictions. As city editor of the *Journal* he seemed to be a "liberal"—an inexact term, but that is the way we thought of him. There was always a shadow of doubt, though. Some of his closest personal friends were outspoken right wingers—supporters of Senator Joseph R. McCarthy.

In 1962, when the Journal Company bought the *Milwaukee Sentinel*, Harvey became the *Sentinel*'s executive editor. Irwin Maier, the company's chairman, had decided that the *Sentinel* should continue to represent the right wing of political thought, as it had under the ownership of the Hearst Corp. Harvey seemed to become a passionate conservative. He made the decision to endorse Senator Barry Goldwater for president in 1964.

What is the answer to this seeming contradiction?

In its obituary, the *Sentinel* said that Schwandner was "enigmatic." Wade Mosby thought so, too. He wrote:

> Harvey was about as tight-lipped as they come. He had plenty of words for sluggish reporters, but I doubt if you will find any staffer who knew one damn thing about how Harvey felt about anything. In a sea of liberal-minded reporters, Harvey was an enigma, an observer, a man with a dour look that could be used to discourage unwanted questions.

Bob Wills worked for him at both papers. He wrote:

> Harvey approached life with a puckish sense of humor that kept his reporters and copy editors guessing. Was he a conservative or a liberal? Not even his editorial writers knew for sure.

Jack Thompson said that he didn't know, either:

> I personally have no idea what Harvey's politics were. It wasn't until he moved to the *Sentinel* that he was in a policy-making position. Even then he didn't have much choice. Irv Maier wanted the *Sentinel* to be the conservative voice, and Harvey went along. I do know he tried to get Con Eklund to leave the [*Journal*'s] Washington bureau and be the *Sentinel*'s editorial writer. Con turned him down—in part, he told me, because he couldn't see himself writing "Hearst-type" editorials.
>
> I don't recall that Harvey played a significant role in the *Journal*'s fight against Joe McCarthy. That was directed by Don Ferguson, then editor of the *Journal* and president of the Journal Company. It was carried out in the editorial columns by Lindsay Hoben and Paul Ringler.

Bob Fleming and I wrote most of the news stories about Joe McCarthy, and I should know how Harvey felt about McCarthy if anyone did. What I do know is that as a *Journal* editor he encouraged the writing of stories that were critical of McCarthy. Fleming and I both wrote long investigative stories, the kind that start with the assumption that the subject did something wrong and it was up to us to expose him. Bob wrote about Joe's dubious claims to military service. I wrote about the money and favors he got from Texas oilmen. Harvey supervised and encouraged the writing of both stories.

There could be two non-political explanations for this. He might have been anti-McCarthy because the paper had taken this position and he was loyal. That's what he seemed to do at the *Sentinel*.

But I think he might also have been doing it because he thought that McCarthy—politics aside—was a liar and a charlatan. He hated phonies, and I think he had decided that McCarthy was one. He seemed to me to have his heart in the fight against Joe. I do know that we reporters always thought that McCarthy was lying, and it was our job to catch him out. Harvey seemed to share that view.

"I know Harvey was not a Republican," said Rick Wing, "and certainly not a conservative Republican. Was he a Democrat? I doubt it. He was a man who was interested in politics, thought it was important, thought it deserved extensive coverage. He wanted this coverage to be impartial, but he left that pretty much to the reporters covering politics—Bayley, Fleming, Bechtel and me. He was an independent, politically."

Wing said that in the contest between Socialist Frank Zeidler and Democrat Milton J. McGuire for mayor, however, Harvey was definitely not impartial.

"I covered most of that campaign, and it was clear to me that Harvey was all for Zeidler," Wing said. "He disliked McGuire. When McGuire ran an ad that insulted the Milwaukee police department, Harvey was delighted that we could publish a news story—an honest, straight news story—that made McGuire look foolish."

Harry Sonneborn was one of those who moved from the *Journal* to the *Sentinel* with Harvey in 1962. He said he did not think Harvey "changed his political stripes" when he moved to the *Sentinel*. He wrote:

> At the *Journal* he often complained about reporters who let their own political slant creep into their stories—the use of loaded words, for instance, or the amount of space devoted to one side and not the other. Reporters who left reporting to work in political jobs only proved to him what he had known all along.

His political stance was determined by the issue in question, not by a party line. In 1964, the presidential campaign was well under way when Irwin Maier, the all-powerful chairman of the board, walked over to see Harvey. The *Sentinel* had come down editorially on the conservative side of several of the issues of the day.

"I hope you're not going to wind up endorsing Barry Goldwater," Maier told Harvey. When the company acquired the *Sentinel* two years earlier, Maier had directed both editors to be independent and make their own policy.

Harvey said nothing. As the days went on, though, he realized that, issue by issue, there was no question that the *Sentinel* point of view—Harvey's point of view—largely agreed with Goldwater's policy and differed from Lyndon Johnson's.

Harvey directed that an editorial endorsing Goldwater be written, and when it was edited and ready for print, he took it to Maier, believing always that one should not surprise the boss.

Maier was not happy about the choice, but he did not interfere.

Sonneborn said that Harvey would have resented any effort to label him politically, but that he was always a conservative when it came to fiscal and economic matters.

But for William R. Bechtel, the change that he observed in Harvey after Harvey took over the *Sentinel*'s editorship was profound. He wrote:

We all know how this transformed Harvey, that delightful, elfish curmudgeon of an editor we had all admired. Those who left before I did would not recall how he built a concrete block wall across our joint *Journal-Sentinel* office in Madison to keep me from ever again reading *Sentinel* reporter Dick Bradee's copy, and noting, as I did after Senator Wiley's famous 1962 press conference ("You keep your damn nose out of my business") that Bradee's story bore no relationship to the story carried in the *Sentinel*.

"*Sentinel* copy is *Sentinel* property and is not to be read by *Journal* employees," read the message on Bradee's teletype. Lindsay Hoben wrote to warn me that I had "risked the wrath of Harvey Schwandner." The workmen with the cement blocks came soon after, and I almost suffocated in my new little cell.

Was this the Harvey I knew? It was as though Boston lawyer Joseph Welch had turned into Gen. George Patton.

As you all know, there were dozens, hundreds, of similar episodes, which caused many to ask which was the real Harvey. It was suggested that he had been this way all along, that throughout those great *Journal* years, "they never asked me for my views." Con Eklund has anecdotes on that—how he and Harvey, as "the two liberals," would debate Oliver Kuechle and J. Gordon Hecker, the two reactionaries, at poker games back in the 1940's. That was Harvey I.

But we musn't turn serious. Harvey was always a great jokester, and most of us treated the great transformation as a good in-house joke.

I agree with Bill Bechtel that Harvey seemed to change when he went over to the *Sentinel*. It was in 1963—three or four years after I left the *Journal* and shortly after Harvey had transferred to the *Sentinel*—when I got into an argument with him at a dinner at the Spauldings' house in Mequon. I said that the idea of assigning liberal and conservative roles to the two papers was hypocritical and he got so angry with me that he stamped out of the house, dragging Gerry, before we had finished dinner.

But we were friendly again 10 years later when an odd thing happened in San Francisco. He was there representing the *Sentinel* at the annual convention of the American

Society of Newspaper Editors. I had assigned my students in a reporting class to the convention, and as part of that coverage, I asked Harvey to be interviewed. These were eager students, enthusiastic about the prospect of becoming journalists. Harvey shocked them.

"It's a lousy business," he said, or something like that. "It's about as exciting as selling insurance, and insurance pays better. Get out of it before you start."

The students thought that he might be joking, but he stuck to his cynical posture, bitter to the end. They didn't know what to make of it, and neither, to tell the truth, did I. What I wonder now is whether he had been embittered by viewing the *Journal* through the windows of the *Sentinel*. He had been promoted, but to a paper that was forced to play second fiddle, and from the outside, we at the *Journal* could be seen as arrogant, even smug. It may have soured him. Or was he playing a game?

Stanley Zuckerman has always been puzzled by his instructions when Harvey dispatched him to cover a story in Georgia, but the story may constitute additional evidence that Harvey was apolitical. Zuckerman wrote:

> I moved up to labor reporter in September, 1960. I was in Harvey Kitzman's office learning something about the United Automobile Workers [of which Kitzman was regional director] when a call came that I was to get back to the *Journal* office immediately. A riot had broken out on the campus of the University of Georgia in Athens following an attempt to register two black students and thereby integrate that all-white institution. I got back to the office quickly, and Harvey called me in.
>
> He told me that, since I had worked in Georgia, they wanted me to leave that afternoon to cover the story that was developing. In light of the prolonged and dramatic confrontation at the University of Alabama the previous year, when Gov. George Wallace

stood in the doorway of the university to deny
entrance to the first black student, Harvey expected
similar events in Athens.

He sliced the air slowly, vertically, with his right
hand, and said: "We are going to play this right down
the middle."

"But Harvey," I said, "the U.S. Government is
trying to enforce the law of the land. The Supreme
Court has said that state universities cannot deny
entrance to people on the basis of their race. Where
is the middle in this story?"

"I don't know," he said without any change in his
stony gaze. "But it's in there somewhere, and you'd
better find it."

In his *Once a Year* story about Dick Davis, Harvey
devoted one paragraph to politics:

His [Davis's] interests are wide. He devours
sports and politics, for instance, and has often written in those fields. Politically, and perhaps largely for
argument's sake, he now is often left of Henry Wallace, although once he was to the right of Alf Landon.
Liberalism came upon Davis sometime during the
depression, just when is not clear, and just what
brought it about has not been determined. At any rate,
Davis is capable of changing his mind.

That might be taken to say that Harvey did not regard
Dick Davis's politics as a defining characteristic. What is
certain is that, while he might not have agreed with Davis's
political views, his admiration for Davis as a reporter, a
writer and a human being was undiluted.

Chapter Eight

PRAISE

Once in a while, most reporters got a note from Harvey saying something good about a story he or she had written. Praise from Harvey was rare and always welcome. I am sure that many of us have some of those memos stashed away somewhere.

The one I remember best was the result of a morning on rewrite. I was a political reporter, but the *Journal* did not believe in idleness. If nothing very important was going on in the field of a specialist, he or she was often assigned to rewrite. Because politics was seasonal, I did a lot of rewrite.

The city desk, about which the news room revolved, was U-shaped. Harvey was in the center, facing in. Across from him, on an angle, was the assistant city editor, who answered the phone and assigned the callers to rewrite men or to other reporters in the room. Bill Radloff, who had been a fast, accurate rewrite man, was the assistant city editor during most of the 1950's. On Harvey's right was Agnes Dunn, the secretary, who often took calls from beat reporters capable of dictating stories without the assistance of a rewrite man. Behind Harvey on the right was the police rewrite man, usually Sammy Benyas, a veteran police reporter and a lightning-fast writer. On the left, down from Radloff, were the other two rewrite men.

Harvey was at work before anyone else, somewhere between 5 and 6 a.m. He would cut up a copy of the *Sen-*

tinel, the morning paper, and attach these clips to the assignment slips he or his assistant made out for everyone on the staff. This is my story:

> When I got in that morning I saw that as a rewrite man I was assigned to two major stories that were expected to break out of the city hall. This was no surprise, as I had been the city hall reporter before I was a political reporter; I knew the territory.
>
> Our deadline for the final edition, the one that would go to subscribers in Milwaukee County, was 12:30 p.m. My two big stories didn't break until noon. Meanwhile, I had picked up another page one story out of the county building and that was still coming in when the others broke. So for about 40 minutes I was writing three stories at once—a paragraph of one, a paragraph of another, and a paragraph of the third, so that the flow to the copy desk was even. Harvey was snatching the paragraphs from my typewriter as I finished each one. It was exciting, the adrenalin was flowing and I never worked faster in my life. We went five or 10 minutes over deadline, which we could do on important stories, and it was a big letdown when the last page went in.
>
> When I came back from lunch, there was a note in my box in Harvey's familiar handwriting: "Anyone who can handle 'Budget,' 'Council' and 'County' is a good man."

I still have that memo. Jim Spaulding, the medical reporter, has one, too. He wrote:

> I think of a memo Harvey wrote on the usual half sheet of copy paper.
>
> I saved it because it was a fragment of precious praise from someone who was sparing with praise. I had begun medical reporting for the *Journal* just a few months before, and John Hirschboeck, the Marquette University medical dean, wrote the paper a letter saying I had become a good medical reporter (surely

an exaggeration, but much appreciated, as was intended) and this reached Harvey. He wrote me a memo (I quote from memory, but one doesn't forget such magic words) saying, "What's more, it's all true."

Tom Blinkhorn didn't get a memo, but he got a smile. He remembers exactly why. He wrote:

It happened on the Izzie Pogrub murder case. I forget the year. Izzie ran a local restaurant near the *Journal* (it was in a hotel and a lot of local hookers hung out there). He had apparently squealed about highjacking meat or something, and many of us who covered police in those days knew from the experts that a contract was out on old 300-pound Izzie.

One day shortly before deadline, a call came in from the Safety Building that a body had been found in a ditch in Mequon and it was believed to be Izzie. I was near the city desk. Harvey asked me to get out to Mequon as fast as I could to find out for sure. O'Brien was on rewrite and was asked to do the front page story for the final edition. I got out to Mequon in record time and was able to confirm from a deputy sheriff that the huge, bloody mess in the ditch was Izzie.

Because of this, I guess, I was assigned to cover Izzie's funeral. It was a big media event in those days with lots of reporters, photographers and camera men. But the family was so angry about the coverage of the murder that they were determined not to let press people into the synagogue for the final rites. I remembered that at such Jewish ceremonies it was appropriate to wear a hat. I had one, put it on and walked past the assembled news throng into the funeral area, where there were lots of rough-looking characters. I kept my hat on and tried to merge into the crowd.

Someone outside, though—maybe a competing reporter—spilled the beans and a hunt began for the *Journal* reporter who had managed to slip inside.

About the same time, the family was asking for volunteers to carry the casket to the graveyard. I volunteered, since I had my hat on, pulled down low, and since I knew if I stood around there I might be found out.

So my big claim to fame in those days was that I helped carry Izzie to his grave and wrote about it. One of our photographers caught me in the act and sent the photo to Harvey who, when he next saw me, beckoned me over to the desk, pointed a finger at the picture of me in the hat, straining under the load, and he smiled. It was a grand day. I had arrived at the *Journal*.

What Stuart Hoyt treasures is a sort of half-compliment. He wrote:

Harvey was very sparing with compliments. Nowadays anyone who does a good job gets mentioned in a long list of kudos in the monthly *Newsroom News.* The one compliment that Harvey paid me has stayed with me always.

It went something like this: "How could a good reporter like you do a damn fool thing like that?"

I was so pleasantly taken aback by the first part of that sentence that I was able to overlook the rest.

One theory that emerges from these anecdotes is that Harvey would modify his approach to suit his assessment of the situation or the individual.

Hale Champion wrote:

I was lucky with Harvey from the outset. No obits, no tongue-lashings, just occasional skepticism embodied in a hard look or a laconic question. Ed Bayley, with whom I had worked in the Madison press corps, was both my mentor and my sometimes queasy sponsor at the *Journal*, and that made my life with Harvey easier right from the start.

Most of the time at the *Journal*, I covered city hall, although I filled in enough on rewrite—sometimes early rewrite before going to the hall—to get a full view of Harvey at work and some of my peers at bay.

Although a few of them thought so, Harvey was not a bully. He did not stretch anything out—especially punishment or unpleasantness. If it had to be, it was always quick, sharp and over in a flash, except for the red in the neck that often lingered like an afterglow.

Bob Wills raised a question that neither he nor anyone else answered: "You had to ask how much of his sternness, how much of his ferocity was sincere? How much was play-acting, done to dramatize a point?"

Robert Wells, who later wrote a history of the *Journal*'s first 100 years, had been the assistant city editor until he took over the paper's New York bureau in 1949. He wrote:

After I left it [the assistant city editor's slot], I realized that I had disliked it thoroughly and I have been thankful ever since that the temptation to go east prompted me to leave it. But my dislike for being at the bottom of the bureaucracy instead of at a typewriter wasn't because of Schwandner. Working for him was a challenge all right, but we got along fine. He always treated me fairly—then and later. I have the impression that this was not always the case. A considerable percentage of those who worked under Harvey wound up hating him and felt he treated them shabbily. They probably were right in some cases, but my feeling has always been that, if you did your job right the first time, you got along just fine with Schwandner as city editor.

Sometimes you got along all right even when you screwed up.

I still remember a morning after an election, one of those times when we worked most of the night and then showed up early the next day after a few hours of sleep. I was assigned to write one of the lesser election stories and I turned it in. Back it came from

Harvey, pointing out some stupid error—forgetting to say who won, maybe, or what office was involved. I wrote a new lead, correcting that error but making another one just as dumb. Back came the copy. Finally, on the third or fourth try, I got my weary brain in gear and turned in an acceptable story. But I never heard a word from Harvey about my incompetence, which surprised me. On the other hand, I'm sure a few more mornings like that and I might have been looking for another job.

Although compassion on Harvey's part surprised people, such acts were not infrequent. Rod Van Every tells of one of these:

Poor as church mice, we reporters could not afford to park our cars in a parking lot. We parked them on the street in two-hour zones. We knew the cops' timing and habits. So it was possible with two trips to your car during the noon hour to remove two sets of blue chalk marks. In the winter slush you spun the wheels.

One day Harvey was in emergency need of a reporter. The city room was almost empty. But there sat Harry Pease. Harvey strode over to him and started to give him the assignment.

"But, Harvey," says Harry, "I gotta check my car."

"Well, first things first," says Harvey.

An even more remarkable example of forbearance on the part of the hard-boiled city editor was during the two weeks before John Pomfret went off to the army. Pomfret wrote:

I was 17 years old when World War II ended and I missed military service. In 1950, when the Chinese entered the Korean War, I was quickly called up by my draft board. In the two weeks between getting my notice and reporting for basic training, my friends at the *Journal*, most of whom were veterans swept up in a wave of nostalgia, undertook an almost continuous farewell party. The hangovers were katzenjammers and the alertness of the staff deteriorated. One friend, a copyreader who had been an artillery sergeant, came in one morning, punched his timecard and dropped it into the suggestion box.

Schwandner endured all of this patiently, but I knew he would be glad to see me go. On my last day, he walked over to say goodbye.

"Thank God you're leaving," he said. "Now I can get a paper out." He paused and I swear that I saw his eyes mist up. "Come back safely," he said.

Two years later I did.

Schwandner drew me aside to a quiet place in the newsroom.

"Look," he said, "the law says I have to give you your old job back, if you want it. But the reporter who is on it now has been doing it longer than you had when you went away. I don't think it would be fair to him to take him off it. If you'll go back on general assignment, I'll give you the first good assignment that opens up."

I agreed.

I spent the next six months covering murders, fires, boring speeches and other people's beats on days off and vacations. Then the reporter who had been covering labor for years left the paper for the golden fields of public relations with a big Milwaukee brewery. Labor was an important assignment in highly-unionized Milwaukee and I didn't think that I would get it. After all, I'd only been a reporter for two years.

I should not have doubted Schwandner as a man of his word.

"Do you know anything about labor?" he asked.

"No," I said.

"Well, you do know the difference between the AFL and the CIO, don't you?" (This was before they had merged.)

"No," I said.

"Good," he said. "You'll be impartial. You're the new labor reporter."

A relaxation of Harvey's militance was noted by Larry Osman:

On occasion, but not often, Schwandner would try to undo a particularly harsh "Ask Harvey" dressing-down for a reporter's mistake by strolling over to the reporter's desk after deadline and telling him of the importance of accuracy, but adding: "We (desk people) should have caught that, too."

Pomfret was the beneficiary of such a stroll. He lived to tell this tale:

The desk which I was given when I arrived at the *Journal* was next to that of John McGuire, a balding, white-haired, pink-faced, puckish Irishman. He had been a police reporter for years, but now was assigned to cover the suburbs. He did this by telephone and had become a master at exposing corruption in some of the towns that surrounded Milwaukee, mostly by artfully working sources he had never met face-to-face.

I was given the desk by accident; it happened to be unoccupied. But it turned out to be a lucky break for me. McGuire took an instant liking to me, as I did to him. He never was too busy to coach me in the techniques of reporting and the mysteries of the *Journal* city room, not least of which was how to deal with the mercurial Schwandner.

One morning Schwandner summoned me. I could tell by the bright red color of his face that there was going to be trouble. He got up from his desk and standing within inches of me in the middle of the news room chewed me out mercilessly for the alleged deficiencies in a piece of copy that he kept waving in my face.

I stood there mute as the tirade continued. It seemed endless and I sensed that all work had stopped as the staff watched and listened. Finally Schwandner wound down.

"Have you got anything to say for yourself?" he asked.

"Yes," I said. "I didn't write that story."

Without another word, Schwandner spun around and sat down at his desk with his back to me.

I walked back to my desk, bewildered and flushed with embarrassment.

"What was that all about?" McGuire asked.

I told him. As I did, I grew angry at the injustice of it all. "By God," I said, "I'm going over and tell that bastard what I think of him."

I started to get up. McGuire put a restraining hand on my arm.

"Son," he said, "as you travel on through life, there are two things that you should remember. One, it is a waste of lather to shave a horse's ass. Two, there are 100,000 laundry workers in America and one of them might be you."

Thus was I saved from a confrontation that might have brought my newspaper career to an abrupt end.

A couple of hours later, after deadline, Schwandner stopped by my desk. He didn't mention the incident. He just made some small talk. But I knew it was an apology from a man who at bottom was fairminded.

Bill Radloff was Harvey's assistant city editor for 11 years, and saw him from a different angle than most of us:

There is one story about Harvey Schwandner that is known only to me. It is probably unbelievable to those who see him as one of those legendary city editors who specialized in brow-beating, raking over the coals or simply ruling his cringing, cowering staff by instilling in them a never-to-be-forgotten fear. It isn't the Harvey Schwandner I knew and worked with from

1946 to 1960—first as reporter, then rewrite man, then assistant city editor.

My judgment about Harvey is based on experiences with three other city editors—Herman Ewald of the old *Wisconsin News,* George Tracy of the old *Sentinel*, and Arville Schaleben, who preceded Harvey as city editor of the *Journal.* So I have a perspective of sorts to fall back on when I perceive Harvey as the most meticulous, hard working and instructive city editor I knew. Compared with Herman Ewald, he was a gentle soul with a deep and abiding compassion for his fellow man, including all the befuddled reporters who crossed his demanding standards.

My short story about Harvey tops everything you would or wouldn't expect of any city editor, let alone him. My wife, recovering from an illness, had a chance to spend two weeks in Florida one winter with her mother and sister, taking our three-year-old son with her. With my whole-hearted agreement, she would leave our infant daughter at home in my care. I had been the assistant city editor less than two years when I asked Harvey if I could take a two-week vacation.

"Why in the winter?" he asked, sensibly. "Going to Florida?"

"No," I replied. "My wife and son are going and I'm staying home with our infant daughter."

"You should have a vacation, too," he said. "Listen, why don't you go with your wife and son? Leave the baby with my wife and me. We'll take good care of her."

When my jaw returned to its natural alignment I thanked him, of course, and explained that having reared three children of their own, he and his wife deserved a vacation from kids. I was certain that the baby would be well cared for in their hands but all the plans had been made, et cetera. He nodded, shook his head and smiled.

Tough guy? Hard to get along with? Not once while I was reporter, rewrite man or his asistant, did he utter a harsh word to me. At the risk of seeming too self-assured, I believe that our relationship was based primarily on mutual respect. And several other members of his staff could make that same statement.

Bill continued:

> The volunteer baby-sitter story has trip-wired another personal relationship story. One year when raises were passed out by Wally Lomoe, mine was the same as that given to the rewritemen. I knew that because Van Every, then on rewrite, told me he was upped by ten dollars a week and, as assistant city editor, so was I. I knew it wouldn't do any good to complain to him [Lomoe] because he could be very stubborn.
>
> One day Harvey came over to my desk and said, "Wally Lomoe is worried about you. Something wrong?" I told him that a hard-working assistant city editor shouldn't be on the same pay raise level as other members of the staff; that, if Lomoe or he didn't like my work, didn't think I was doing a satisfactory job, I wouldn't mind going back to rewrite. I spoke quietly but firmly. I was trying to make a point and Harvey knew that I was.
>
> "Take it easy," he said. "I don't want another assistant."
>
> About two or three weeks later, out of the blue, Lomoe called me into his office and gave me another ten dollar raise. "I'm not in the habit of doing this," he said, "so don't use this tactic on me again." Then he smiled. Of course, Harvey had suggested the additional raise.
>
> I suppose it's inevitable that Harvey Schwandner will be remembered by most of his associates as an SOB. But every teacher has his method and style. Harvey was a teacher and had his own style and method. He didn't suffer fools or fatheads gladly and more power to him, I told myself.

Marion Wilhelm, too, says that "sometimes he was tender-hearted." She said that in 1948 she asked Harvey for an extra day off so she could go by train to visit her mother, a school teacher, in a hospital in Washburn, Wisconsin. Thursday was her regular day off, and she wanted Friday, too. Marion continued:

> "Why two days?" asked Harvey.
> "It's four hundred miles," I said.
> "Can't someone else visit your mother?"
> "She's all alone."
> "What's she doing in the hospital?"
> "Traction."
> Harvey didn't like crybabies—male or female. He was marking up the overset that hadn't made it into the final edition. "We have a NEWSPAPER to get out!" he said. I thought that meant "no."
> It was December. The Ashland Limited inched forward through a snowstorm, the chill winds of a Wisconsin winter blasting me in my sleeping car. When I awoke in the early light of dawn, the train was frozen to its tracks in Green Bay—or was it Oshkosh? Thursday morning—my day off!—and I wasn't going to make it to Ashland until two hours before the return run to Milwaukee . . .
> I grabbed a taxi to Washburn from the frozen platform—ten miles still to go. My mother was surprised to see me—yes, my visit lasted twenty minutes—and so was Harvey Schwandner when on Friday morning I appeared right off the Ashland Limited at 8 a.m. sharp!
> He was standing near the assignment boxes when I showed up on time, and he looked genuinely surprised: "I thought you were taking Friday off," he said.

Marion thought that Harvey tried to make up for this misunderstanding by giving her some good assignments soon after that.

Stanley Zuckerman's experience in seeking a pay raise from Harvey told something about the way the *Journal* management regarded its employes, but it also showed Harvey's softer side. He wrote:

After four months at the *Journal*, I was increasingly in debt. I went to Harvey.

"Harvey," I said, "I understand you are the one who sets salaries here, and I need a raise."

"You just got here," he said.

"I know," I said, "but I had no idea of the cost of living here compared to Georgia. If I weren't working overtime almost every night, I'd be starving, and I can't work day and night any more."

"Are you saying that we took advantage of you, that we hired you too cheaply?" he asked.

"It's just that I've begun to find out what other people are getting around here who don't have nearly the responsibility you've given me," I said.

Those icewater eyes narrowed, the bank clerk's mouth pursed, and the neck stiffened slightly below the line of the two-dollar haircut.

"What," he asked, "is your theory of compensation?"

"You should pay a man what he's worth," I said.

"You'll never make a manager," he said scornfully. "You pay a man what you can get him for."

But I did get a big raise for those days—$15 at Christmas and another $7.50 in June. Arv Schaleben told me about the raises, but when I went up to Harvey to thank him he turned away as if embarrassed, and never responded.

Chapter Nine

SUMMING-UP

Harvey Schwandner was a strong person and he left behind him strong opinions about his place in the world of newspapers.

"Harvey was one of the country's best newspapermen," said Bob Wills. "He perhaps did not gain the recognition of his peers that he deserved because of the kind of man he was—modest, unassuming, more interested in putting out a good newspaper daily than in building a name for himself."

"The Harvey Schwandner that I knew," said Joe Shoquist, "was a complicated man who is some ways was a contradiction to himself, and I have to search for words to describe him—gruff, rude, ill-tempered, even cruel at worst; witty and humorous, earnest, perhaps caring, when he wished to be. He certainly was hard-working and dedicated to his job, a loyal company man, a good editor in a *Front Page* sort of way. Basically, I think Harvey was a shy and introverted man, not very confident in himself, who developed a personality and manners to mask some of his inadequacies. Don't we all?"

"I never thought he was the world's greatest city editor," said Rick Wing, "and I don't now, but I wish to God there were a few like him around today, because today he might be the world's best.

"Harvey did love his job. He loved the *Journal*, and by and large he loved the people who worked for him. As a city editor, though, was he a great journalist? Did he have great ideas, find new ways to go after stories? I think not. I think he was a traditional city editor, acting in a solid, unspectacular way. He had the loyalty of his people because he was fair, was open to discussion, and he backed his staff. He ran a tight ship, no question.

"I'm just saying that I don't think he rose above the level of city editors around the country at papers of the same size and reputation. I always liked Harvey; I never feared him. He was a good man, a good newsman, a good editor, but his reputation is perhaps larger than the actuality."

Larry Osman's judgment was much like that of Rick Wing.

"Certainly he was among the last of the breed of demanding, abusive taskmasters," Osman said, "but I have never been totally convinced that he was a great newspaperman. His crew, at least the bunch of which I was a part, was made up of hungry, slightly overage former GI's, and we accepted his leadership because we had wives and babies to feed. Who knows, we might have been as good or better with a different hand, which I think Schaleben had had earlier, although I did not work under him as city editor."

Hale Champion saw Harvey as a man who was more interested in the "institution"—the *Journal*—than in personal ambition.

"I only spent 18 months with Harvey and that was 45 years ago in a life of various occupations in an even wider variety of settings," Hale said.

"He is, however, a more vivid figure than many of the other ghosts of the past. He was certainly the ablest and most interesting of the half dozen city editors I dealt with in the newspaper business, or perhaps I should say simply that he was the only one of notable capacity and interest.

It strikes me now, from the fact that my most recent activity has been the teaching of management, that he was a notably effective manager of people and process beyond the narrow category of city editors.

"He was a man of his institution. Within his culture, within the *Journal*'s boundaries, he reflected standards, integrity and commitment, even occasional flashes of imagination and humor—the kind of internal manager who makes all kinds of institutions function best. You couldn't have had a much better city editor for a paper like the *Journal*—a very good newspaper—but I suspect that like some very good local wines, he wouldn't have travelled well. In his case, that was no problem. He wasn't interested in exploring the larger world."

Jack Thompson wrote: "Harvey was a complex character. He was on rewrite when I came to the *Journal* teamed on the state desk with Don Trenary (another fine talent and, unlike Harvey, a patient teacher of young reporters). I recall how amazed I was when I first read a feature story of Harvey's. It was beautifully written, full of wry twists and chuckles. It seemed so out of keeping with Harvey's dry, abrasive exterior. I wonder if he might not have enjoyed life more if he had remained a writer. I feel that as city editor he was driven."

Jim Spaulding, too, was surprised and impressed by Schwandner's skill as a writer and reporter.

"Preparing one time to write a column on lightning strikes, I came across a story in the *Journal* library about lightning striking at a park in Milwaukee during a baseball game," he wrote. "The reporting was meticulous and the writing, vivid. I looked for the byline—Schwandner. It was the only byline of his I ever encountered. I think that the *Journal* rarely gave bylines then. It might give reporters the notion that they were important."

Bob Wells wrote about the organization of the *Journal* desks—what he called "nearly autonomous kingdoms."

This was a theory he developed while writing his history of the *Journal*.

"In the days when Harvey was czar of the city desk, the *Journal* news room was a group of nearly autonomous kingdoms," Wells said. "Schwandner ran the city desk; Don Trenary, the state desk; Russ Lynch, the sports desk. Lomoe probably had some influence, especially when the subject was trains, ducks or circuses, but the straw bosses pretty much ran things. It was our good fortune that Schwandner as well as Trenary and Lynch had been reporters.

"Newspaper people are divided into only two categories—reporters and what I still think of as copyreaders. When Schwandner moved up to the mostly mythical job of assistant managing editor, the copyreaders took over and have generally been running things ever since.

"Harvey knew the difference between a well-written story and hack work because he had been a fine writer and a competent reporter himself. That was before my time, of course, but I judge from the clips I've read. Writing standards are not very high at newspapers, including the *Journal*, but the percentage of editors who knew a well-crafted piece from the hack variety was fairly low. (Not quite as low then as now, I think, but that may be old age creeping up on me.) When I started writing articles for the old *Saturday Evening Post* and various other magazines, I discovered that such matters as transitional phrases between topics loomed much larger with those editors than with those in the newsroom, where meeting a deadline had a much higher priority than graceful prose."

John Pomfret summed up this way:

"I know that there were disagreements about Harvey's pedagogical skill. I thought that he was a great teacher. The lessons were brief and sometimes unpleasant, but they were clear and they stuck. Harvey didn't have a lot of time to spend with young reporters. His was a hands-on operation. Most of the time, he was working flat out. He had to deal with a goodly number of inexperienced newcomers and a staff of vastly varying capabilities. He didn't have time for patient elaboration. His fast, direct, no-nonsense approach suited the situation.

"And what did he teach us?

"First, that the work that we did was important. Cynicism (differentiated from skepticism) is the cancer of newsrooms. Reporters who don't believe that what they do matters soon don't do it well enough for it to matter. With Harvey, you were never in doubt. You knew that he cared immensely—even about the least important story in the paper. And you had better care, too, or you weren't going to be around very long.

"Second, that a little office politics went a long way. He was task-oriented. If you tried to play games with him, all you got back was a fishy stare.

"Third, that it was the facts that mattered. He was a reporter's editor. He knew how hard it was to find out what was really happening and he loved diggers. You were entitled to your opinions, provided you kept them out of your stories. To him, your views were no better or worse than anyone else's and didn't interest him. It is when I read in today's newspapers all of those sloppily reported essays masquerading as news stories that I miss Harvey the most.

"Fourth, he taught that accuracy is important even in small things.

"I think that his staff and his newspaper owed a lot to a man who taught those lessons. And we shouldn't forget that the local report for which he was responsible may have been the best in the country. Certainly, his city was a better place because he worked there."

Jim Spaulding reflected on Harvey's place in the world of newspapers: "Here was a man, nondescript in many respects, not what could be called charismatic, but he shaped the craft ethics and the lives of a generation of journalists on one of the top newspapers in the United States.

I suspect the corporate world is full of Harvey Schwand-ners, men (and maybe today, women as well) who rise to positions of influence because they are able and forceful; they set standards for the generation of people who admire them and to some extent fear them.

"Once you understood what it was Schwandner wanted, what we admired and lived by—provided, of course, you believed in those ideas, too—working for him was a real joy."

And finally, I quote from the letter Gerry Schwandner, Harvey's widow, wrote to me when she learned that this project was afoot:

"I knew Harvey a long time—sixty years—since our first date in high school.

"He was then a young man with printers ink on his hands. He set type by hand at the *Brillion News,* where he worked after school and Saturdays.

"He was a loving, caring person with a dry sense of humor. A private family man, proud of his three bright children. He was not a disciplinarian, only by word. To them: 'If you get into trouble, you'll be front page.'

"His work, the newspaper, was top priority. He worried about the paper and the community.

"You know, I knew he wrote well. I wanted him to write. After his retirement, I suggested he write a book. He said, 'The book I want to write I can't.' I never pressed him for the 'why?' Was it Fourth and State and community? We had an interesting happy life together.

"I'm sure Harvey will be looking over your shoulder when you write this, to see if it's OK. We don't want you to receive a note, 'See Harvey, pls.'"

Maybe he was looking over my shoulder. On the night of February 24, 1992, after working all day on these stories, I had a dream. I was back in the *Milwaukee Journal* city room, still covering politics. For a week or so I had wanted to talk to Harvey about something important, but I hadn't had the courage to confront him.

It was just after the 12:30 p.m. deadline, in the few minutes before Harvey had to go up to the composing room to handle last-minute crises. He walked over to my desk in the northeast corner of the room. He was wearing a green shirt, a brown sleeveless sweater and a bow tie. His voice, when he spoke, was neither friendly nor unfriendly.

"I hear that you want to talk to me," he said. "Go ahead."

Then, for the life of me, I couldn't remember what I wanted to ask him, and he was still standing there when I woke up.

NOTES

FOREWORD

vii HARVEY SCHWANDNER WAS   The daily circulation of the *Milwaukee Journal* rose steadily from 281,467 in 1946 to a peak of 373,657 in 1963. It stayed above 360,000 until 1970, when it began to decline. It was 275,632 in 1990. Sunday circulation was 314,298 in 1946. It peaked at 561,851 in 1968. In 1990, it was 505,351. The *Journal*'s Sunday edition throughout the period was a morning newspaper; the daily was an afternoon paper.

ITS NATIONAL REPUTATION   Senator Joseph R. McCarthy (1908-1957) was elected to the Senate as a Republican in 1946 and re-elected in 1952. Beginning in 1950, his charges—largely unfounded—that members of the Truman adminstration and employees of the State Department were Communist sympathizers or worse made him the most controversial figure of the era.

viii MORALE IN THE   Harry J. Grant, later the *Journal* Company's chairman, was a businessman with the soul of a reporter. When a group of movie executives came to complain about critical reviews, he threw them out of his office—and their ads out of the newspaper. A remote figure at the time of this narrative, he spent most of his time in Florida fishing from his yacht.

ix HARVEY WILLIAM SCHWANDNER   The population of the village of Brillion in 1910—two years after Schwandner's birth—was 998.

CHAPTER 1: ANXIETY

3   LATER, COVERING   George Lockwood later became
the *Journal*'s picture editor.

6   SOME OF US   *Front Page* is a newspaper melodrama by
Ben Hecht and Charles MacArthur that was first staged in
1928. It has been revived many times since in the form of
plays, musical comedies and movies. It is set in Chicago in
the gangster era of the 1920's, and the tough, hard-drinking,
cigar-smoking, cynical newspapermen have hearts of gold.

SOMETIMES HARVEY'S OUTBURSTS   Several words
are used in the newspaper business for stories that rely more
on the writer's ingenuity and style than on his possession
of hard facts. Among other things, they have been called
"think pieces," "dope stories," "backgrounders" and
"explainers" or, in an expression that indicates the skepticism with which they are sometimes regarded in the trade,
"thumbsuckers."

FOR A WHILE   Robert H. Fleming was a *Journal* political reporter until 1952, when he left to work in the Chicago
bureau of *Newsweek*. He later became ABC News bureau
chief in Washington, D.C., deputy press secretary to
President Johnson, and legislative aide to Rep. J. J. Pickle
(Dem., Texas).

9   IN 1948, HARVEY WROTE   Richard S. Davis (1890-1964)
is considered the *Journal*'s greatest reporter, an especially
fine writer and one of its most colorful characters. After
abandoning a promising career as a concert singer, he wrote
features and news stories for the *Journal* from 1918 to 1961,
specializing in criticism of music and drama. Upon his retirement in 1961, the *Journal* published a selection of his writ-
ings under the title, *The Best of Davis*.

CHAPTER 2: ENTERPRISE

12   HARVEY TOOK ONE LOOK   The *Tribune* headline
appeared the morning after the day of the 1948 presidential
election. The outcome was still in doubt when the *Tribune*

had to go to press. Its editors apparently thought it inconceivable that Thomas E. Dewey, the Republican nominee, who had run comfortably ahead in the polls, could lose. They took a chance and lost. A photograph that appeared on almost every front page the next day showed a victorious, grinning Truman waving a copy of the *Tribune*.

15   WHAT EXCITED AND ELATED   Milo Bergo was a *Journal* reporter who covered police and suburban news.

ANOTHER SUCH INCIDENT   Dan Hoan, a Socialist, was mayor of Milwaukee from 1916 to 1940. The *Journal* consistently and vainly opposed his policies and his candidacies.

18   I CAME BACK   Arville Schaleben joined the *Journal* staff as a reporter in 1929, became city editor in 1943, assistant managing editor in 1946, managing editor in 1959, executive editor in 1962 and associate editor in 1965.

18   BOB'S STORY CONCERNS   William J. Manly was the longtime real estate editor of the *Journal*. He also covered urban affairs. Henry J. Maier, a Democrat, was mayor of Milwaukee from 1960 to 1988. Although he feuded with and fumed against the *Journal*, he was willing to cooperate when it seemed to be to his advantage.

21   IT DID, ALONG WITH   John Reddin was a *Journal* editorial writer specializing in politics and foreign affairs. He became chief editorial writer in 1972 and died in 1977 while abroad on assignment.

CHAPTER 3: SUPPORT

23   THE SAME WAS TRUE   Wallace Lomoe was managing editor of the *Journal* at the time of Wing's anecdote. He came to the *Journal* state desk in 1928 from the *Superior Telegram*. He became state editor in 1929, news editor in 1945, managing editor in 1946, executive editor in 1959. He retired in 1962.

25   LIZ COVERED THE   Donald J. Abert was employed by the *Journal* as a copywriter in the promotion department in

1928. He married Barbara Grant, daughter of Harry J. Grant, in 1936. He was business manager in 1948 and became executive vice-president and general manager in 1961 and chairman of the board in 1977.

CHAPTER 4: ACCURACY

26 WHEN HARVEY QUESTIONED   Arthur Ochs Sulzberger, scion of the Ochs/Sulzberger family that controls the *New York Times*, held a number of jobs at the *New York Times* before becoming its publisher in 1963. On his watch, the *Times* reached new heights of journalistic excellence and business profitability. He turned the publisher's reins over to his son, Arthur Ochs Sulzberger, Jr., in 1992, while continuing as chairman of the parent company—a post he first assumed in 1973.

28 LATER, REVIEWING MY STORY   Andrew W. Galvin was an experienced and reliable reporter who covered politics and public affairs.

ONCE AT OUR HOUSE   George Groh was a general assignment reporter from Texas, a fairly new arrival at the time.

29 ALTHOUGH I HAD BEEN   James G. Wieghart, *Journal* reporter 1958-62, held various newspaper jobs, including several years as editor of the *New York Daily News*. He also held congressional staff jobs, and handled press relations for the office of the special prosecutor in the Iran-Contra investigation (Lawrence Walsh).

31 MY FIRST ENCOUNTER   H. Paul Ringler became a *Journal* reporter in 1927. In 1935 he was a news writer for WTMJ. He became assistant city editor in 1943, an editorial writer in 1946, chief editorial writer in 1961 and associate editor in 1966. He retired in 1972.

35 KENNY SMITH WAS ON   Ken Smith became editor of the weekly *Cambridge* (Wis.) *News*, after leaving. He later died in an automobile accident.

36 HE EXPECTED A REPORTER   "Typo" is short for typographical error—a mistake made when setting type or

typing by accidentally striking the wrong key on the keyboard. Before computers took over and eliminated paper copy, reporters were expected to go over their stories and correct them with a pencil.

37   HARVEY SCHWANDNER, WHO   The City News Bureau was a local wire service that provided news of police, courts and local government to the major news outlets in Chicago. Many young midwesterners began journalistic careers at the bureau.

ONCE, ON POLICE REWRITE   The name of police headquarters in Milwaukee was the Safety Building. Some of the criminal courts were located there.

CHAPTER 5: PUNCTUALITY

40   SEVERAL PEOPLE CONTRIBUTED   Neil McKay was a young *Journal* reporter at the time.

"RED ALERT!" SOMEONE   Stow Row gots its name because the newer general assignment reporters who largely populated it had to write a lot of stories that were used as filler to wrap around ads in the huge food and other supplementary sections that the *Journal* was running at the time. These stories often had no time element in them and hence could be "stowed" away by the editors to use as needed.

43   BUT POOR J. PAUL   J. Paul O'Brien covered the federal building and cultivated the friendship of FBI agents. He also did police rewrite. He drank a lot and played cards for high stakes.

CHAPTER 6: PERSONALITY

44   I'M NOT SURE   Jim Taylor was a celebrated fullback for the Green Bay Packers who played on Vince Lombardi's championship teams. He was able to bull his way through seemingly impenetrable opposition.

48   I DID HAVE MORE   J. Gordon Hecker worked in the Sunday department and wrote a column for the Green Sheet, the daily entertainment section.

50　THE YEARS FLY　　　Lloyd D. (Hap) Gladfelter joined the *Journal* staff as a reporter in the early 1920s. He was covering the city hall in 1932 and was there until 1946, when he became a specialist in urban affairs. He retired in the early 1960s.

50　BILLY POHL, OUR　　　William Pohl was a Milwaukee businessman, a cheerful fellow who spent a lot of time at the Press Club.

51　I REMEMBER SOME　　　Bob Hope is the movie comedian. Marshall Field was the Chicago department store tycoon who bought and published the *Chicago Sun-Times*. Edna Ferber was the novelist. She had been a *Journal* reporter for three years just after the turn of the century. Celebrities who came to Milwaukee usually visited the Press Club to sign their names in chalk on slate blackboards that were framed and displayed at the club.

51　I ALSO REMEMBER　　　Schwandner might have been saying "cubit" inch displacement (*Latin, cubitum,* elbow) in a reference to raising the elbow, to drink. The cubit was an ancient measurement of the distance from the elbow to the tip of the longest finger. (Source: *Brewer's Dictionary of Phrase and Fable.*)

CHAPTER 7: POLITICS

52　IN 1962, WHEN　　　Irwin Maier was advertising manager of the Madison *Capital Times* when he joined the *Journal* in 1924 as an advertising salesman. He became vice president and publisher in 1943 and president in 1961. In his last active years, he chose to be the editorial adviser to the editors of the *Journal* and the *Sentinel*. Senator Goldwater, an Arizona Republican, represented the right wing of the GOP in 1964. He received 52 electoral votes to 486 for Lyndon B. Johnson.

53　I PERSONALLY HAVE　　　Laurence C. (Con) Eklund covered politics and the state legislature for the *Journal* from the 1920s until 1947, when he was assigned to Washington, D. C., as a one-man bureau. He retired from that job in 1970.

I DON'T RECALL   J. Donald Ferguson came to the *Journal* as an editorial writer in 1923 and became chief editorial writer in 1927. He became president and editor in 1943 and retired in 1961. Lindsay Hoben joined the *Journal* staff in 1926 and spent several years as a roving foreign correspondent. In 1934, he became the first editor of the Sunday editorial section. He was made an editorial writer in 1938, chief editorial writer in 1949, vice president in 1955, and editor in 1961. He retired in ill health in 1967.

55   WE ALL KNOW HOW   Senator Alexander Wiley (Rep., Wis.), during most of his unsuccessful 1962 re-election campaign, was kept in Washington by his handlers. They apparently feared that he had lost his grip and that public appearances would show it. When the strategy became too obvious, a press conference was scheduled at Madison. Wiley, alarmed and confused by dogged questioning about his position on Medicare, at one point shouted at Bechtel: "You keep your nose out of my business and I'll keep my nose out of your business." When Bechtel learned that the story about the press conference that appeared in the *Sentinel* bore little relation to that filed by the *Sentinel*'s reporter, he wrote a note to the *Sentinel* asking why. The wall went up shortly thereafter.

56   WAS THIS THE HARVEY   Joseph Welch was the courtly New England lawyer whose question to Senator McCarthy in the 1954 televised Army-McCarthy hearings ("Have you no sense of decency, sir?") turned the tide of public opinion against McCarthy. Army Gen. George C. Patton was a swashbuckling leader of tank battalions in World War II, whose bullying of soldiers under his command became a public issue.

AS YOU ALL KNOW   Oliver Kuechle was the *Journal*'s sports editor in the 1950s.

57   HE TOLD ME THAT   Gov. George Wallace was a leader in the fight against racial integration in the 1960s. He served two terms as governor of Alabama, and in 1968 ran as a third party candidate for president, receiving almost 10 million popular and 46 electoral votes.

58   HIS [DAVIS'S] INTERESTS   Henry Wallace was President Roosevelt's Secretary of Agriculture from 1933 to 1940 and was Vice President from 1941 to 1945. He was a third party (Progressive) candidate for president in 1948, backed by the left wing of American politics, and received a little more than one million votes. Alfred M. Landon was governor of Kansas from 1933 to 1937. As the Republican nominee for president in 1936 against Franklin Roosevelt, he carried only two states—Maine and Vermont.

CHAPTER 8: PRAISE

60   WHEN I CAME BACK   The newspaper term used for the words that Schwandner used to identify the stories that Bayley had handled that day—Budget, Council and County—is "slug." Every story in a newspaper is identified by a one-word slug. If a story is a running story—that is, one that continues for more than a day—it usually will be identified by the same slug day after day.

64   ONE DAY HARVEY   Harry Pease covered science and space exploration for the *Journal*.

CHAPTER 9: SUMMING-UP

75   IN THE DAYS WHEN   Russell Lynch was an investigative reporter in the early 1920s, describing himself as a "hatchet man." He became sports editor in 1932 and wrote a column that was often controversial. In 1956, he began covering natural resources and the environment on a full-time basis, said to be the first such assignment in the nation.

THE DAVIS PROFILE

Following is the text of Harvey Schwandner's profile of Richard S. Davis as it appeared in *Once A Year*, the annual magazine of the Milwaukee Press Club, for 1948:

RICHARD S. DAVIS
A Temperamental "First Fiddle"

Like the corner saloon and sauerbraten, Mister Richard S. (for Smith) Davis of the *Milwaukee Journal* is a firmly entrenched Milwaukee institution. As a drama and music critic of the *Journal*, he wields a formidable influence in the city's cultural life. Davis does not stop at mere culture, however. He has written on a thousand topics in his time, and his by-lines, if laid end to end, would probably stretch from Milwaukee to Chillicothe.

Dick Davis, that's the name, and surely he is Milwaukee journalism's outstanding character. He looks, and sometimes acts, like a bishop. Years of good living and a snooty attitude toward exercise have given him a rather portly figure. He wears with distinction a gray and wispy mustache. His hair is gray and thin on top. His plastic-rimmed spectacles have thick lenses. He has shrewd brown eyes that have a boyish sparkle when he laughs. His nose is Roman. All in all, Davis presents a patrician figure, and at times there is evidence that he knows it. That is to say, he permits himself to "ham" on occasion. He owns a rich baritone voice, which is frequently raised in anger against the things he feels to be wrong and in defense of what he feels to be right.

Once Davis was hot for being an opera singer. He went into journalism instead, but he retained the opera singer's temperament, all to the benefit of journalism. His explosions of either anger or laughter in the *Journal* city room no longer greatly startle the inhabitants. A newcomer, however, will be alarmed to see Davis get red in the face, flail the air with his arms, and spout invective like a human Vesuvius. Davis in anger is indeed an awe inspiring sight. Sometimes his anger courses inward. On these occasions he pads up and down the city room, hands stuffing his pockets, a black scowl knitting his graying brows. He looks as cross as a tomcat with no lady friend to comfort him. And woe to the innocent who seeks to ask him some mundane question at these times.

Much of the time the Davis approach to a story is emotional. It is this quality which makes him a great reporter, one of the greatest in the country. He can, however, dig facts with the best of diggers, especially when he is mad. Indeed, Davis is a journalistic triple threat—he can write marvellous feature stories, he can read copy and write headlines, and he can write a straight story. The latter, however, frequently proves a difficult chore for him. He just can't help being Dick Davis.

His interests are wide. He devours sports and politics, for instance, and has often written in those fields. Politically, and perhaps largely for argument's sake, he now is often left of Henry Wallace, although once he was to the right of Alf Landon. Liberalism came upon Davis sometime during the depression, just when is not clear, and just what brought it about has not been determined. At any rate, Davis is capable of changing his mind.

His desk is a mess. Piled high are books, magazines, concert programs, notes from old assignments, newspapers, letters from admirers, letters from guys who speak frankly of assaulting him, clippings—all these and more. But the Davis mind is neat, sharp, orderly. When he sits down to write a story, he is all concentration. Like a surgeon with a scalpel, Davis works neatly with his typewriter. He hunches over the machine, punching expertly but slowly. His copy is a delight to copy readers. Seldom is there so much as a comma out of place. He thinks ahead. He knows exactly what he is going to say in the next paragraph. He is a precision writing instrument. He slaves at his work, struggling, searching, probing for the right word, the delicate phrase, the right ending. The Davis stuff is remarkable because he is willing to sweat like a butcher over it.

As he writes, he runs his fingers through what is left of his hair. He is tousled after a session with the machine.

Most of the time Davis is in a high good humor. He is an entertaining companion, full of droll stories, witty observations on almost any subject, racy dialogue that leaps and bounds like a greyhound after a rabbit. He is a downright lovable cuss much of the time. On occasion, however, black moods come upon him. Then, indeed, he is nothing less than Edgar Allen Poe. He speaks dismally of the future of the nation. He fears for civilization itself. Capitalism he gives up with a despairing wave of his hand. For journalism he has but a sigh and a heave of his ample midriff. At these times his features, ordinarily wreathed in cherubic smiles, fall into the grim and dour physiognomy of a pall bearer. On these occasions, the urge to throw him down a well is great indeed.

There are also times when he is extremely cross with his associates. When he feels that an associate has been guilty of being a journalistic dummkopf, he scowls and glares at the culprit until the poor fellow is convinced that assault and battery will follow. Davis also can be as chilly as a dowager toward his fellow journalists on occasion.

It is all part of being Dick Davis, a complicated human being, you understand.

A perfectionist himself, Davis demands perfection in music and the theater. His tastes are high. He thinks well of John Charles Thomas, but has only a snort for Bing Crosby. A creature like Mae West, for example, he disposes of in a one-paragraph review dripping with arsenic. For the finest of the theater, Davis has warm, lavish praise. But let a darling of the stage turn in a bad performance and Davis will pounce on him with obvious relish. He can be relentless with what he feels to be mediocrity.

As a youth, Davis dreamed of a career in opera. The son of a Milwaukee Methodist minister, Davis began nibbling at culture by entering Lawrence college at Appleton, Wis. He was a lively student, ah, yes. He didn't stay at Lawrence long.

Davis himself is not too clear about that Lawrence interlude. All he has ever said for the record was contained in his column, "And So It Goes," on January 10, 1940:

"In the memorable year of 1909—or was it 1910—anyway, in some memorable year, yours for old Lawrence was duly enrolled as a student and ever since then has considered the college the sanest of all educational institutions, because it had the sense—oh, well, boys will be boys."

Soon after that he began his musical training, taking lessons in Chicago, New York and then Paris. His Paris teacher, the famed Jean de Reszke, thought well of him. A yellowed clipping from the *Milwaukee Journal* of May, 1914, tells glowingly of how a young Milwaukee baritone sang the baritone aria from Pagliacci in one of de Reszke's famous Little Theater concerts.

Shortly before the outbreak of World War I, Davis returned to New York to continue his studies. Unable to enlist in the United States army because of his poor eyesight, Davis worked in a shipyard at Newark, N.J., when the United States entered the war. His mother's death in the spring of 1918 called him back to Milwaukee.

Davis had been thinking realistically of his future as an opera singer. He had a strong suspicion that the heights were not for him. He had a dread of being just another good singer. All this mental process, rather unusual in so young a man, caused him to sour on singing as a career. Then he heard of an opening on the old *Evening Wisconsin*. The late, beloved John R. Wolf was then city editor of the paper. Davis decided to take a crack at the newspaper business.

He liked it. In September, 1918, he moved over to the *Journal*. He started as city hall reporter. From that spot he moved to the assistant city editor's desk, and then to the copy desk. In 1921 he began reviewing plays and concerts, also continuing his work on the copy desk. He was able to do that by coming to work an hour early, writing his reviews before sitting in on the desk.

It was not long before Davis' flair for feature writing was put to work by the *Journal*. Then began the remarkable flood of Davis stories, and his by-line became a household word in Milwaukee. He covered national political conventions, the big prize fights of the roaring twenties, the Kentucky Derby, the John Dillinger funeral, the trial of Al Capone, the funeral of President Roosevelt—there you have just a sampling. For years he wrote a column in the *Journal* Green Sheet. Every year he went to New York for a searching look at the new plays which might perhaps some day grace the stage of the Davidson or the Pabst. During the war Davis undertook a task that required a lot of work. Each week, in the Green Sheet, he presented a review of the hometown news for a GI addressed as "Dear Joe." It made a lot of friends.

In 1946 the *Journal* received the "courage in journalism" award of Sigma Delta Chi, national professional journalism fraternity, for its articles on squalid housing in Milwaukee's Negro district. Most of the articles were written by Davis.

He had become deeply interested in the plight of Milwaukee's Negroes. Davis was assigned to the Negro housing problem after writing a moving editorial on the beauty of the voice of Marian Anderson, famous Negro contralto, and the injustice of the Negro housing situation. The editorial was one of the finest that ever graced a newspaper. It had fire and indignation and deep sincerity. It had obviously been written at white heat by an artist. One could not read the piece without a moistening of the eye and a quickening of the pulse.

Last year Davis wrote a witty and barbed chapter on Milwaukee for *Our Fair City,* a book about the shortcomings of 17 major American cities, edited by Col. Robert S. Allen.

While Davis has often taken Milwaukee over his knee and whaled it mightily, he still loves the town and has refused the siren calls of New York newspapering. The truth is, Davis is well off in his home town. He lives on Lake drive. He has many good friends. He is respected. He is reasonably well off.

The stock market in 1929 burned his fingers. Davis is droll about his stock market experiences. He has been heard to say, "People come from miles around to get my advice on investments." While it can hardly be true that the stocks Davis buys go down automatically, there seems to be some mysterious economic law at work on his holdings. Davis, of course, despaired long ago of ever getting rich, so the behavior of his stock is really of no moment to him.

Occasionally Davis is called upon to make a speech. This he does uncommonly well. He is articulate, forceful, commanding. What's more, he loves to make a speech. Sometimes the Lawrence college alumni call upon him for a few words. One time they waited for hours for him to show up. He didn't. He had just forgotten about it, he explained, shame-faced, the next day.

Seldom does he lift his rich baritone voice in song. Occasionally, when he is with friends and spirits are running high, he will sing like a good fellow. He has sung at weddings for good friends. Sometimes when he is strolling in the city room and life is good, he will hum and sing softly, beaming all the time.

And at other times, when there is a crisis, the opera singer comes out in him again, full blown and wonderful. Like the occasion not long ago when a makeup man telephoned him from the composing room and began tentatively, "Say, Dick, that review of yours is about three inches long for page 15. Could you trim it?"

Davis turned cherry red, shouted into the phone, "No, ——. I won't take a ———— word out of it." And bang went the receiver. Everyone in the city room turned around to watch. Davis stood up, legs apart, a veritable Horatio fending off an onslaught, his eyes flashing fury, his features reflecting magnificent rage.

It made a wonderful scene. And the old maestro knew it.

ARTHUR OCHS SULZBERGER
WRITES ABOUT THE JOURNAL

The following is the Foreword to *The Milwaukee Journal: The First Eighty Years* by Will C. Conrad, Kathleen F. Wilson and Dale Wilson. University of Wisconsin Press (Madison and Milwaukee, 1964).

The *Milwaukee Journal*, lively as a golf ball and clean as spring water, is a newspaper with a chapter all its own in the history of American journalism, but I have a complaint to make about it. The complaint is that in the year I spent on the newspaper as a reporter I was kept so busy writing obituaries about freshly deceased Wisconsinites that I did not have time to get to know enough of those still drawing breath.

Of course, other people have had complaints about the *Journal*, too. Government officials in Milwaukee complain that they cannot twitch a civic muscle without the *Journal* knowing about it. Politicians of every political party have complained that being flayed alive is a most uncomfortable sensation. And I imagine that there is hardly a reader of the *Journal* who has not complained at one time or another about having some of his favorite theories or prejudices or preconceived notions jostled so hard that he had to think them through again.

There are only a handful of newspapers in this country that have become synonymous with the cities where they are published. The *Journal* is one of them. To think of Milwaukee without the *Journal* is like trying to think of New York without Broadway, San Francisco without the Golden Gate, Washington without the Capitol—clearly impossible.

Perhaps more that any other newspaper in the country, the *Journal* has become identified with the health and growth of its community. It has fought against its natural enemies—corruption and crime and civic lackadaisicalness. It has also fought just as hard *for* things—for civic integrity, for tolerance, for awareness.

But the story of the *Journal* is, I think, considerably more than the story of the relationship between a newspaper and a city. It is the story, most of all, of free thinking. The most important contribution of the *Journal*—the contribution that really goes beyond journalism—is that it has broken down shibboleths and clichés about the American mentality, most particularly the "Midwestern mind."

There is a caricature about the Midwest that is accepted as a true portrait in many places in the world. In broad strokes, the Midwest is drawn as provincial, withdrawn, isolationist, stolid. By rights, therefore, the *Journal* should be interested only in its own backyard and have its mind made up in advance on political issues and candidates. Since the truth about the *Journal* is exactly the opposite, it has helped change some of the quick stereotypes about the Midwest.

The *Journal* is a great local paper—but it is not a provincial paper. The whole world is its beat. It is a paper with opinions as strong as hot mustard, but no politician or party can assume support by the *Journal* in advance. It has a richness of heritage but has never been tied down by tradition—even when its own readers objected to its maverick qualities. Its story is worth reading, and remembering.

Arthur Ochs Sulzberger

CONTRIBUTORS

Armstrong, Alicia (1926-). Worked for papers in Dubuque and Davenport, Iowa, before joining *Journal* staff as a reporter in 1952. Wrote news and features concerning the zoo, medicine, religion and other subjects. Retired in 1988.

Bayley, Edwin R. (1918-). The author. *Journal* city hall, legislative and political reporter 1945-59; executive secretary to Gov. Gaylord Nelson (Dem., Wis.) 1959-61; Peace Corps, White House staff and State Department under President Kennedy 1961-64; vice president National Educational Television 1964-69; professor and dean Graduate School of Journalism UC—Berkeley 1969 to retirement in 1985. Author: *Joe McCarthy and the Press* (1981).

Bayley, Monica (1919-). Director, news bureau, University of Wisconsin-Milwaukee 1952-59; editor and writer, US Office of Education, Washington, 1962-64; editor, McGraw-Hill, New York, 1965-69; editor and writer of ethnic cookbooks, travel guides, Determined Productions, San Francisco, 1969 to retirement in 1984. Wife of the author.

Bechtel, William R. (1923-). Joined *Journal* staff as a reporter in 1950 from *Grant County Independent* of Lancaster, Wis. Worked on state desk, as religion reporter, political reporter and Madison bureau chief. Left in 1963 to become staff director for Senator Gaylord Nelson (Dem., Wis.). Later a member of the cabinet of Gov. Patrick J. Lucey (Dem., Wis.), federal chairman of the Upper Great Lakes regional commission and director of the state of Wisconsin's office in Washington. Retired in 1986.

Blinkhorn, Thomas (1935-). Joined the *Journal* staff as a reporter in 1959 from the *Cincinnati Enquirer.* Covered police, city hall, business and economics, then became an editorial writer. Left for World Bank in 1970. Currently environmental adviser for India.

Cattoi, Louise (1894-). Emigrated from Italy to Hurley, Wis., in 1900. After a year of normal school in Duluth, taught in one-room school in rural Minnesota for two years. Left University of Wisconsin in 1919 after less than a year to accept job offer as *Journal* reporter at $18 a week. Pioneer in developing coverage of women's groups as they dealt with substantive issues, rather than as society news. When she retired in 1963, she was making $150 a week. Honorary member of the Milwaukee Press Club's Hall of Fame.

Champion, C. Hale (1922-) Reporter, United Press(Madison bureau), *Journal* (city hall reporter), *Sacramento Bee, San Francisco Chronicle, Reporter* magazine. Press, executive secretary Gov. Edmund G. (Pat) Brown (Dem., Calif.), 1958-60; California state director of finance, 1961-66; vice president, financial planning, University of Minnesota, 1969-71; vice president, finance, Harvard University, 1971-76; under-secretary, HEW, 1977-79; executive dean, JFK School of Government, Harvard, 1980-87; chief of staff, Gov. Michael Dukakis (Dem., Mass.), 1987-88; lecturer, JFK School, 1989-91.

Dewey, Viola (Vi) (1914-). Reporter, *Wisconsin Rapids Tribune,* 1936. Joined *Journal* staff in 1937 on society desk. Forced to resign in 1941 when she married Edward Dewey, *Journal* copy editor. Rehired by *Journal* in 1961 and worked in women's news department until retirement in 1979.

Dishon, Robert L . (1921-). As member of 5th special amphibious brigade, landed on Omaha Beach at H-hour,

D-day, June 6, 1944. Joined *Journal* staff as reporter from *Columbus* (Ohio) *Dispatch* in 1955. Moved to *Sentinel* in 1962 when the Journal Company bought it. Covered urban affairs for *Sentinel* and later for *Chicago Daily News.*

Doyle, Robert J. (1914-). Joined *Journal* staff as reporter from *Sheboygan* (Wis.) *Press* in 1939. Copy editor, war correspondent in the Pacific and Europe, New York bureau chief, Madison bureau. Left in 1957 to become press relations director for Northwest Airlines. Later owned a public relations firm. Assistant to director, Wisconsin State Universities System, 1962-71; director of university relations and assistant to president, University of Wisconsin System, 1971-80; part-time work for UW System to 1985.

Eifert, Carl A. (1926-). Joined the *Journal* staff as a rewriteman in 1957 from the Madison bureau of the United Press. State desk, Madison bureau, Madison bureau chief. Left in 1966. Held a number of posts as editor, teacher. Press secretary for Senator William Proxmire (Dem., Wis.) 1970-76. Since 1989, with Catholic News Service in Washington.

Harris, Michael (1922-). *Journal* reporter 1946-48; reporter *New Orleans Item* 1949-51; reporter *San Francisco Chronicle* 1951, editorial writer 1988.

Hibbard, Bill (1927-). Joined the *Journal* staff as reporter in 1952 from *Dubuque* (Iowa) *Telegraph-Herald.* Travel editor, 18 years; auto editor, two years; ski writer, 20 years. Retired 1990. Freelance writer and photographer.

Hoyt, Stuart (1922-). Joined *Journal* staff in 1951 as a reporter; added assignment as garden editor 1955; copy editor on telegraph (foreign and national) news desk 1962-88.

Kloss, Jerry (1925-). Joined *Journal* staff in 1949 as reporter; reporter and feature writer 1949-53; writer in Sunday Feature Department, music and drama critic, 1953-1960; wrote bi-weekly column "Slightly Kloss-eyed" for the Green Sheet, the daily entertainment section, 1960 to retirement in 1989. Book of collected columns published in 1984.

Koshollek, George (Sam) (1925-). Joined *Journal* on photo-lab staff in 1949 from the *Stevens Point* (Wis.) *Journal*. Shortly thereafter became staff photographer. Retired in 1987.

Krueger, Jack E . (1914-). Joined *Journal* staff as reporter in 1937. Transferred to radio news desk in 1938. Headed news department of WTMJ, the *Journal's* radio station, from 1942, incorporating television news when TV was introduced into Wisconsin in 1947. Retired in 1980.

Lohmann, Lawrence C. (1926-). Joined *Journal* staff in 1951 as reporter from *Syracuse* (N.Y.) *Herald-Journal*. Covered the federal building, city hall (15 years), labor (eight years) and the suburbs, transporation, police and metropolitan affairs. Retired in 1986.

McLean, John (1924-). Joined *Journal* staff in 1949 as a reporter. Became education reporter in 1950. Left in 1956. Later editor, *East Hartford* (Conn.) *Gazette;* managing editor, *Connecticut Life Magazine;* executive director, Community Renewal Team of Greater Hartford, an antipoverty agency; various posts with the U.S. Department of Housing and Urban Development, lastly as manager of the Hartford office handling all HUD programs in Connecticut.

Mosby, Wade H., Jr. (1917-). Started on the police beat at the *Sheboygan* (Wis.) *Press*. Joined *Journal* state desk staff after 33 months service in the USAF in the south Pacific during World War II, during which he rose from private to captain. State editor, New York bureau chief, feature writer, editor of the Green Sheet (the daily entertainment section) and simultaneously the TV/Screen Magazine. Later wrote a tri-weekly Green Sheet column, "We Like It Here."

Retired in 1981. Founder of the Whitefish Bay (Wis.) Community Band.

Osman, Loren (Larry) (1917-). *Journal* reporter, farm and feature writer, editorial writer 1948-82. Since retirement, free lance writer. Author of two books on agricultural history.

Pilarski, Laura (1926-). *Journal* reporter 1949-60. Free lancer in Europe. Chief correspondent, McGraw-Hill World News, 1965-88. Author: *They Came from Poland* (1969) and *Tibet: Heart of Asia* (1974).

Pomfret, John D. (1928-). *Journal* reporter and briefly editorial writer 1949-62. Reporter the *New York Times* 1962-66. Then business positions with *Times*, lastly as executive vice president and general manager for eight years. Retired 1988.

Radloff, William H. (1914-). Reporter and rewriteman on old *Wisconsin News* and *Milwaukee Sentinel*, 1937-42. After wartime service in Pacific as special agent and counterintelligence officer, joined *Journal* staff in 1946 as reporter. Was successively rewriteman, assistant city editor and feature editor. As assistant city editor under Schwandner, often acted as buffer and pacifier. After early retirement in 1969, became assistant story editor at Twentieth Century Fox. Subsequently, freelancer writing fiction and television scripts. Published poet.

Shoquist, Joseph W. (1925-). Joined *Journal* staff 1955; news editor 1964-67; managing editor 1967-86. Dean, College of Journalism, University of South Carolina, Columbia, SC, 1986 until retirement.

Sonneborn, Harry L . (1919-). Joined *Journal* staff in 1940 as copy editor. Was assistant news editor when he succeeded Harvey Schwandner as *Journal* city editor in 1959 when Schwandner was made assistant managing editor.

Became managing editor of the *Sentinel* in 1962 when the Journal Company bought it and Schwandner became its executive editor (later, editor). Became executive editor of the *Sentinel* after Schwandner retired in 1975.

Spaulding, James C. (1921-). Reporter, United Press, Detroit 1946; reporter and city editor, *La Grande* (Ore.) *Evening Observer*, 1947-48. Joined *Journal* staff as reporter 1948; became medical reporter about 1951. Left *Journal* in 1971 to join faculty of Graduate School of Journalism, University of California, Berkeley, teaching science writing. Retired 1987. President, Stonegate Winery, Calistoga, CA, since 1973.

Thompson, John H. (1909-). Joined *Journal* state desk staff 1936 from *Watertown* (NY) *Daily Times.* Successively state editor, telegraph desk copy editor, New York bureau chief, reporter, editor of Sunday editorial section, editorial writer (for 12 years), "Contact" section editor, and ombudsman. Retired 1974. Prime mover and sparkplug of *Journal* news and editorial employees alumni association and author of its quarterly newsletter.

Tonne, Fred L . (1924-). *Journal* staff photographer and occasional writer 1949-1967. Since 1975 has operated police equipment sales business with stores in Milwaukee and Minneapolis and sales operations throughout the Midwest.

Van Every, Rod (1915-). Got his start in the newspaper business as (simultaneously) editor, reporter, columnist, sports writer, layout editor, advertising solicitor and part-time janitor of the *Tomahawk* (Wis.) *Leader,* a weekly. Covered general assignments and police for the *Wisconsin State Journal* in Madison, 1941-45; navy 1945-46; joined *Journal* staff 1946. Covered most beats. City editor for seven years. Retired 1977.

Wells, Robert (1918-). After working on newspapers in Ohio and World War II service in the Navy, joined *Journal* staff as reporter in 1946. Assistant city editor 1946-49, New York bureau chief 1949-56, humor and book editor/columnist. Retired 1984. Much published freelance writer. Author of 18 books, including the centennial history of the *Journal*.

Wiggins, David (1921-). Joined *Journal* staff as reporter in 1954 from *Omaha World-Herald*. Left in 1960.

Wilhelm, Marion Bell (1925-). *Journal* reporter, 1947-51; foreign correspondent in Mexico and Central America; Mexico City bureau chief of *Chicago Tribune* 1951-65 and correspondent for numerous news organizations; public affairs specialist and Congressional correspondent for U.S. State Department, 1966-78. Freelancer.

Wills, Robert H. (1926-). Joined *Journal* staff as reporter in 1951 from *Duluth* (Minn.) *Herald & News Tribune.* Named *Journal* assistant city editor in 1959 when Schwandner was named assistant managing editor. Named city editor of the *Sentinel* in 1962 when it was purchased by the Journal Company and Schwandner became its executive editor (later, editor). Named editor in 1975 after Schwandner retired. Vice chairman of Journal/Sentinel Inc., publisher of the *Journal* and senior vice president of Journal Communications Inc. until retirement.

Wilson, Ellen Gibson (1919-). Joined *Journal* state desk in 1943 from *Kenosha* (Wis.) *Evening News.* Transferred to the city side as a general assignment reporter and feature writer, and became the first full-time welfare reporter. Left the *Journal* in 1962 for a public information post with the Department of Health, Education and Welfare in Washington. Has lived in Great Britain since 1964. Author of scholarly books on British and American involvement in the African slave trade.

Wing, Elizabeth (Liz) Block (1931-). *Journal* reporter, 1953-54; housewife and free lance writer, 1955-60; researcher, Yale

University Library, 1960-63; information and finance officer, Colorado House of Representatives, 1964-70, and manager of Colorado Eugene McCarthy campaign committee; retail public relations and advertising, 1971-78; marketing manager, Wisconsin savings and loan associations, 1978-87; marketing consultant to financial institutions, 1987-.

Wing, Merrick S. (Rick) (1927-). *Journal* reporter 1950-57. Administrative assistant to Representative Henry S. Reuss (Dem., Wis.), 1957-60; Yale Law School class of 1963; lawyer, Denver, 1963-70, and LaCrosse, Wisconsin (birthplace), 1970-80; assistant professor, mass communications department, University of Wisconsin-LaCrosse, 1980 to retirement in 1991.

Wittenberger, Avery (1912-). Got start in newspaper business as reporter, columnist, advertising salesman, printer, pressman and janitor on *Preston* (Minn.) *Republican,* a weekly. Joined *Journal* staff as reporter in 1943 from *LaCrosse* (Wis.) *Tribune.* Eight months later was assigned "temporarily" to cover the Milwaukee County Courthouse which he did until his retirement in 1977.

Zuckerman, Stanley (1933-). Joined the *Journal* staff as reporter from *Columbus* (Ga.) *Enquirer* in 1960. Left in 1963 to be executive secretary to Gov. John W. Reynolds (Dem., Wis.). Foreign service U.S. Information Agency in Congo, Korea, Belgium, Mexico, Canada and Brazil. Currently senior adviser to USIA acting director.

INDEX

(Harvey Schwandner is abbreviated as HS; "n" = note;
"c" = contributor biographies.)